Endorsements

M000166762

I love tools for my relationship with God, and Doug Addison delivers an amazing one in his new book, *Hearing God Every Day: The Supernatural Ways God Speaks to Us*. Doug has a unique connection to language and expression that will take you on a journey into understanding the supernatural ways that God speaks to you! When you learn how to hear from God you learn how to thrive in life, and Doug is giving you bite-sized ingestible pieces to do just that. Read this book!

SHAWN BOLZ
www.bolzministries.com

Doug Addison's latest book, *Hearing God Every Day: Understanding the Supernatural Ways God Speaks to Us*, is another masterful insight into the ways that God reveals Himself to us every day of our lives. Doug skillfully takes the reader through the different and various ways God speaks to us so that we can recognize, respond to, and perceive God's still, small, and audible voice. Hearing God brings wisdom, increased prosperity, and healing to us as we develop a lifestyle of communing with God through prophecy, dreams, and visionary encounters with the myriad angelic messengers sent by God. Learning how to maintain an open heaven empowers us to see and speak to God whenever we need to hear from Him. I am proud to call Doug my friend and I highly recommend him as a prophetic mentor and life coach to everyone who wants to grow in their spiritual understanding of God's supernatural ways.

DR. BARBIE L. BREATHITT
"Ask Barbie" Prophetic Dream Life Coach
Author of *Dream Encounters, Gateway to the Seer Realm, Dream Seer, Dream Interpreter*, and *The A to Z Dream Symbology Dictionary*
www.MyOnar.com

The "Pro" is at it again. Doug Addison is one of the most consistent prophetic voices in the body of Christ today. As an authentic prophet he has the capacity to train others in the very area he walks in. You will find practical and relatable keys in *Hearing God Every Day: The Supernatural Ways God Speaks to Us*. Come up to the next level and grow in intimacy with God for yourself!

JAMES W. GOLL
God Encounters Ministries
GOLL Ideation LLC
Author, Singer, Communications Trainer

I have known Doug Addison for many years and it has been a great honor to watch him grow in his influence to empower individuals all over the world to walk in greater prophetic revelation!

Doug operates powerfully in his gifting to not only communicate the heart of the Father and release timely prophetic words, but he also demonstrates the true mark of a prophet—equipping the saints to hear from God! The effects of this cannot be overstated—an empowered generation who can recognize God's voice is a formidable force of light and love!

In his new book, *Hearing God Every Day: The Supernatural Ways God Speaks to Us*, Doug shares from his decades of experience to equip you to hear from God and to know how to steward your prophetic words. I believe the application of prophetic words is a missing key for many believers and that this book will give you practical tools and principles to know how and when to follow through on the revelation you receive.

Whether you have never heard the voice of God before or would like greater insight on walking out and following through on the words you receive, this book will be a life-changing tool!

I believe Doug's book will catalyze its readers to greater impact in the Kingdom of God!

KRIS VALLOTTON
Senior Leader, Bethel Church, Redding, CA
Co-founder of Bethel School of Supernatural Ministry
Author of thirteen books including *The Supernatural Ways of Royalty, Heavy Rain,* and *Poverty, Riches and Wealth*

Doug Addison is a prophetic minister called and anointed by God to train, equip, and lead the body of Christ into new dimensions of love, grace, and power. He is a friend of mine whose prophetic ministry I respect and rely upon.

His new book, *Hearing God Every Day: The Supernatural Ways God Speaks to Us*, is a wonderful work that will be a great help to every believer. Jesus said, "My sheep hear my voice," yet many Christians struggle mightily to do so. I encourage all of you to read this book and make its teaching a part of your life. It will be a great blessing to you for years to come.

JOAN HUNTER
Author/Evangelist
TV Host, *Miracles Happen!*
Joanhunter.org

Doug's latest book, *Hearing God Every Day: The Supernatural Ways God Speaks to Us*, is such a gift to the body of Christ and the world. It is a rich treasury of divine wisdom for hearing God's voice and understanding the ways He speaks. I love Doug's love for the Word and teaching the realms of the supernatural that is grounded and founded in the Word of God. This book will not only unlock you into deeper realms of hearing God's voice, but also catapult you into a whole new world of encounter while also helping you to discern and recognize His voice in your everyday life. This book carries a significant impartation and I believe will increase your hunger to know Jesus and hear from Him more than ever before. This book is timeless and one to be referred to regularly in this new era.

LANA VAWSER
Prophetic voice, Itinerant Speaker
Author of *The Prophetic Voice of God*

This book will revolutionize your life. Finally, a book that not only trains you how to hear God's voice but how to discern and interpret the prophetic words you receive and how to actually activate these prophetic words so that you start to fulfill your destiny at an accelerated pace. Often due to lack of knowledge and understanding, most don't fulfill their full destiny as the Word says in Hosea 4:6 *"My people perish for a lack of knowledge."* Finally, the revelation knowledge is here as you fast-forward into your ultimate destiny and high calling you have been yearning for.

Dr. David Herzog
Scottsdale, Arizona
www.thegloryzone.org

Hearing God Every Day

Hearing God Every Day

UNDERSTANDING THE SUPERNATURAL WAYS GOD SPEAKS TO US

DOUG ADDISON

© Copyright 2019–Doug Addison

All rights reserved. This book is protected by the copyright laws of the United States of America. This book may not be copied or reprinted for commercial gain or profit. The use of short quotations or occasional page copying for personal or group study is permitted and encouraged. Permission will be granted upon request. Unless otherwise identified, Scripture quotations are taken from the HOLY BIBLE, NEW INTERNATIONAL VERSION®, Copyright © 1973, 1978, 1984, 2011 International Bible Society. Used by permission of Zondervan. All rights reserved. Scripture quotations marked NKJV are taken from the New King James Version. Copyright © 1982 by Thomas Nelson, Inc. Used by permission. All rights reserved. All emphasis within Scripture quotations is the author's own.

DESTINY IMAGE® PUBLISHERS, INC.

P.O. Box 310, Shippensburg, PA 17257-0310

"Promoting Inspired Lives."

This book and all other Destiny Image and Destiny Image Fiction books are available at Christian bookstores and distributors worldwide.

Cover design by Eileen Rockwell

Interior design by Terry Clifton

For more information on foreign distributors, call 717-532-3040.

Reach us on the internet: www.destinyimage.com.

ISBN 13 TP: 978-0-7684-4554-1

ISBN 13 eBook: 978-0-7684-4555-8

ISBN 13 HC: 978-0-7684-4557-2

ISBN 13 LP: 978-0-7684-4556-5

For Worldwide Distribution, Printed in the U.S.A.

1 2 3 4 5 6 7 8 / 23 22 21 20 19

Acknowledgments

I want to give a special thank you to my wife, Linda, who has loved endlessly and walked with me in ministry for all these years. Linda is a gift from the Lord who helps keep me anchored and grounded; she has been completely supportive of me and endured the long hours of writing and preparation it takes to produce a book and curriculum of this nature.

The message in this book was birthed after a weekend away with some of my friends who helped pull it out of me and get it into an outline form. Special thanks to Elizabeth and Jon Nixon, Stephanie Olsen and Linda Addison for this. And to my Executive Assistant Apryle Borst who has helped free me up to operate in my creativity.

I also extend thanks to my team at InLight Connection who have helped me in their various capacities with keeping this project moving forward—Krista Abbott, Tanya Knobloch, Dee Collins, Arlene Brown, Bev Simons and Joel Maust. Their dedication to helping me get my prophetic words and written messages out to the world is astounding and I am very grateful for their love and support of me throughout this project.

Contents ～

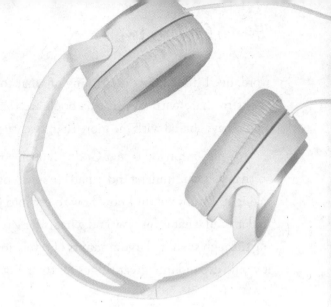

Introduction

I am so excited that you are taking a step toward developing your ability to hear the voice of God. If you picked up this book, then chances are that at some point in your life you have heard the voice of God or received a prophetic word from someone, and wondered what to do with it. Possibly you have not heard God's voice at all, and that is okay too.

Whether you received a prophetic word from someone or if God spoke to you directly, this book will help because it contains practical ways to help you respond to what God has given to you. Too often people will receive a prophetic word from God, but they do not follow through with it, let alone activate it in their lives. I am excited to share some principles and practices that will really help you.

The most common questions I get after training tens of thousands of people on hearing God are: "How can I know if what I am hearing is from God, myself, or the evil one?" Also, "I have received a prophetic word, but I don't know the timing or what to do with it." What I am about to share with you in this book are the things I wish someone would have shared with me more than twenty-five years ago.

My prayer for you is that God will open your spiritual eyes and ears so that you can understand what He is saying to you, and why He is saying it. I want you to know how to get into God's timing so you can understand what is for now and what is for later. Whether you are praying through small or large amounts of revelation, my goal for you is that it would expand into great things for the Kingdom of God.

Is That You, God?

I have been hearing the voice of God all my life, but for many years I did not realize it was God, so I seldom responded to Him. Most of the time, I considered the guidance and insight that came to me as coincidences. Looking back, I now realize that I did experience supernatural things, but never understood them or knew that I should track them.

Because the Christians I knew at that time did not understand me or know how to guide me, I became very wounded and was in and out of church for many years. Even though I had encounters with Jesus, I could not figure out how to change my life. I would go up to the altar over and over, praying for Jesus to save me. It was like I was born again—and again and again!

Finally, in 1987, God got my attention through prophecy. I was in the occult and had gone to a psychic (which I do not recommend). I was backslidden from the Lord and was in desperate need. Then to my surprise, the Holy Spirit spoke to me about my condition right there in the psychic's office! A year later, my sister, who had been in the occult practice with me, gave her life to Jesus. She called me at five in the morning and said that Jesus had awakened her and told her to call me and tell me the very thing He had spoken to me in the psychic's office. I was shocked because I had not told anyone about those words.

I responded to what Jesus said, and my life changed forever! I found a church that offered emotional healing and helped me develop my spiritual gifts. But what I found most helpful was that they nurtured my ability to hear God. Since then, I have been a pastor, church planter, and business owner. I was one of the forerunners of prophetic evangelism in which we use prophecy and biblically based dream interpretation as a means of sharing God's love.

My First Encounter with Prophecy

In 1988, I went to my sister's church because a minister there had the gift of prophecy. He said to my brother-in-law, "You need to lose weight." I thought that was not very prophetic because it was obvious that my brother-in-law was quite heavy. Then he turned to me and said, "The woman you are with is not the one."

I had been with that woman for seven years, and I had come back to God in the process. We were going to get married, even though my friends and pastor did not agree. I knew that she was not in the same place as me spiritually, but I really wanted to be married. I thought I was doing the right thing.

One year later, the woman I married left me and my brother-in-law died of a heart attack. Wow! That got my attention. I ended up divorced and alone, crying out to God. I wanted to hear God for myself.

My Life Verse and Mission

One day I was sitting in my apartment and heard the Holy Spirit say to me, "Isaiah 61." I had no idea if there even was an Isaiah 61 in the Bible. This is what I found when I looked it up: *"The Spirit of the*

Sovereign Lord is on me, because the Lord has anointed me to proclaim good news to the poor. He has sent me to bind up the brokenhearted, to proclaim freedom for the captives and release from darkness for the prisoners" (Isaiah 61:1). I burst into tears because I knew this was my destiny. I cried for about six weeks because God was speaking to *me*—an alcoholic, meth-addicted, backslidden mess!

That was my introduction to hearing God for myself. I went on from there, and still had a lot of ups and downs. But now here I am, decades later, and He has been doing exactly those things from Isaiah 61 in my life.

That experience set me on a journey to learn to hear the voice of God. In 1991 there were no ministry schools or online training like we have today. I read books and listened to teaching tapes, went to conferences, and absorbed a great deal of training. Over time, I moved from hearing God inconsistently and often vaguely, to increased confidence in recognizing His voice.

I began to discover His will for my life, getting accurate prophetic words for others and growing into deeper intimacy with God. But it was not until I did the things I am going to show you in this book that hearing God's voice opened like a floodgate for me.

Prophecy, Dreams, and Destiny

One of my three main areas of expertise is teaching and training in the prophetic gifts. I have given thousands of personal prophetic words to people over the years. I release monthly prophetic words on my website, write weekly prophetic articles on my blog, and release daily prophetic words on the internet.

Another area of expertise is helping people understand their dreams by studying examples in the Bible and with guidance from the Holy Spirit. After interpreting more than 30,000 dreams, I have discovered that many of the dreams we have at night—like flying, having a baby, losing teeth, or showing up with no clothes—can reveal clues about our unique life purpose and point us toward our life dreams.

This discovery led to my third main area of expertise, which is helping people discover their life purpose and move into their destiny. When I would train people in giving prophetic words in the market-place, I realized that a lot of Christians do not know their own destiny! You cannot give away what you do not have yourself.

Many people are having dreams, but there are few who can interpret or understand dreams from a spiritual or Holy Spirit perspective. There are a lot of people receiving prophetic words, but there is not much training on how to respond and how to activate what God is saying to you. I became a certified Life Coach to help people understand and ful-fill what they are hearing from God.

We all can hear God, and God longs for you to hear Him. Learning to hear God's voice is a lifelong process, yet it is simple enough that even a child can do it. One statement Jesus said more than any other: *You must have eyes that can see and ears that can hear.* He was talking about understanding things *spiritually.* Understanding parables and develop-ing your discernment will help you learn how to hear God accurately and understand your dreams and destiny. It is very sad that much of the Christian Church today has let go of the ability to hear the voice of God. I have good news, though! Through the process I lay out in this book, you can be part of the solution.

Foundations for Hearing God

This book is a practical "how to" activation and mentoring experi-ence. This is not a Bible college type of teaching. I am going to fast-track you at times into an accelerated learning process. I am *not* going to try to prove to you that God speaks today. I am assuming you already know and believe this.

Sometimes I will use Bible verses and teaching. I will also use practical activations and stories to build your faith and to make it real for you. Everything I am offering you is built upon the following biblical foundation:

1. The most important purpose for hearing God is to know Him better and help others do the same.

> *I keep asking that the God of our Lord Jesus Christ, the glorious Father, may give you the Spirit of wisdom and revelation, so that you may know him better* (Ephesians 1:17).

God can speak to us in some amazing ways, but it always boils down to knowing Him better. It's also important to understand that just because God might speak to one person more clearly than another, it does not make that person special or better. God loves us all the same.

2. Prophecy and revelation are for encouragement and not judgment. We must be motivated by the Spirit of love in order to build up and not tear down.

> *But the one who prophesies speaks to people for their strengthening, encouraging and comfort* (1 Corinthians 14:3).

The Old Testament is full of examples of judgmental prophecies. The purpose was to get the Israelites, God's chosen people, back on track. So many people today do not have a biblical foundation, so judging them for what they have no knowledge of does not strengthen, comfort, or encourage them at all! Also, the Old Testament prophecies were given before people had the Holy Spirit in them like we do in the New Testament times.

3. We are building our foundation on the love and message of Jesus Christ.

For it is the Spirit of prophecy who bears testimony to Jesus (Revelation 19:10).

I realize that not everyone who will read this book is in the same place spiritually. I promise not to preach or tell you what to believe. I know that some of the things I will be sharing might sound controversial or even stretch you at times, but each is built on a biblical foundation and a lifetime of experience.

4. We can be naturally supernatural.

Very truly I tell you, whoever believes in me will do the works I have been doing, and they will do even greater things than these, because I am going to the Father (John 14:12).

Hearing God does not need to be spooky or mystical. I like to think of the supernatural things of God as being a natural part of our lives. Jesus and His disciples had dramatic supernatural experiences and modeled what we can expect as we grow in our relationship with God.

5. You do not have to be a prophet to hear the voice of God.

My sheep listen to my voice; I know them, and they follow me (John 10:27).

Jesus compared our relationship with Him to sheep that know the voice of their shepherd. While not all people are called to prophetic ministry, or hearing God for others, we can all hear God for ourselves, learn to understand what He means, and know what to do next.

Are you ready to go on a journey into hearing the voice of God?

Believe and Receive

Most people understand that we need to believe in God's promises and receive His love and acceptance. Believing can sometimes be too passive and does not advance God's Kingdom in the proactive way that He wants. We need to go beyond just believing, and move into a proactive lifestyle. Most people are waiting for God to make changes in their lives for them. Jesus says in Matthew 7:

> Ask and it will be given to you; seek and you will find; knock and the door will be opened to you. For everyone who asks receives; the one who seeks finds; and to the one who knocks, the door will be opened (Matthew 7:7–8).

If you want to hear God's voice, it requires believing, asking, and waiting for God to open the door. But Jesus also says that we can seek and knock, which are proactive steps we can take. You are going to discover in this book that there are many practical things you can do on a daily basis that will change the spiritual atmosphere around you. God is speaking all the time and we just need to get in tune with Him and cultivate a supernatural lifestyle.

Get ready to be activated into a new level of hearing God's voice. Whether you are just starting out or a veteran, there is something for you in this book. I am excited that you are taking steps to open the door to hearing God. You are going to be pleasantly surprised!

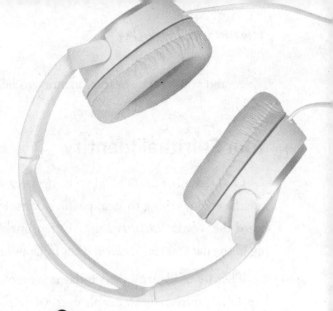

CHAPTER 1

Discovering How God Speaks

Have you ever thought of something, and suddenly you hear a song on the radio that really speaks to what you were thinking about? Maybe you are thinking about someone, and then you hear from that person. Have you ever been driving and feel like you should slow down, and then you see the police? Have you been waiting in the checkout line at the grocery store and have a nagging feeling to move to another line, and then you see the other line move faster?

These are some examples of how God speaks to us. They are not coincidences, but are better described as *God-incidences*. Can you identify with any of them? If so, there is a good chance that you are already hearing God daily and may not realize it. God has placed in you His

DNA, and you have a spiritual identity to hear His voice every day of your life.

Your Spiritual Identity

On December 26, 2009, I woke up after several dreams in which I saw the enemy trying to steal people's destinies. As I prayed about it, I heard the words *"identity theft."* Oftentimes, things that are happening in the natural realm reveal what is happening in the spiritual realm.

The rise of identity theft today is symbolic or prophetic of what is happening spiritually to people everywhere. In the dreams, I saw two covert strategies that Satan is trying to use against people to keep them from seeing, finding, and fulfilling their life purpose and destiny in God: 1) getting us to believe that we are our behavior, and 2) dying too much to yourself and losing your passion. Let's look at each strategy in more detail.

Strategy 1: Satan Wants to Convince Us that We Are Our Behavior

Bad experiences or painful pasts can negatively affect our present. There are forces of darkness that want us to believe that we are the only ones who suffer with these issues and that they are unchangeable. This is simply not true. Too often our sin and emotional baggage gets linked to what we believe about ourselves. In other words, our personality and identity become associated with the things we struggle with.

The strategy of the enemy is for us to believe that we actually are how we feel or behave, which is not true at all. Satan wants you to believe things like: you "are" depressed, unhappy, worthless, unable to change, stupid, a failure ... the list could go on and on. It is important to realize that our feelings and behavior can be changed, and they do not determine who we really are. They might be things that we struggle with, but they are not our identity, or who we are in Christ.

Most people do not see that there is a direct connection between the way they view themselves and their destiny. This includes the things that you may think about yourself at a deep level. You might not consciously believe them, but you find yourself thinking them or saying them about yourself on a regular basis.

For as he thinks in his heart, so is he (Proverbs 23:7 NKJV).

Strategy 2: Satan Wants Us to Die So Much to Ourselves that We Lose Our Passion

Satan wants to steal our identities, taking away any hope for a better future and convincing us we have no purpose for living. When he is able to get us to believe the lies about ourselves in Strategy 1, he then uses Bible verses out of context, as he did with Jesus, to release a second deadly attack against our destinies by getting us to over-respond to our sin.

It is interesting that, while writing about how to find God's will for your life, the apostle Paul says that we must first change our thinking by renewing our minds.

> *Do not be conformed to the pattern of this world, but be transformed by the renewing of your mind. Then you will be able to test and approve what God's will is—his good, pleasing and perfect will* (Romans 12:2).

Renewing your mind involves a principle called *dying to yourself.* There are several verses in the Bible that talk about dying to the sinful nature or "old self" and allowing God to live through us. This necessary process will transform your life from the inside out, revealing your true motives or reasons why you say, do, want, and believe certain things. God wants to heal whatever is not in line with how He sees you, and to replace every lie with the reality about who you are and your life purpose.

Satan wants to get you to take this to the extreme and will try to mislead you to believe that you must die to *all* of your desires and plans. But the truth is that God wants you to be His child and to have authority as His family on the earth. God wants to give you the good things you want and desire, when your motives are lined up with His.

> *Take delight in the Lord, and he will give you the desires of your heart* (Psalm 37:4).

God's Good Intentions for You

A really great thing about God is that He sees us as who we are becoming through His love and power. As He looks at our lives, He knows our past, understands our present, and can see us in the future, all at the same time. His love, mercy, and grace are unfathomable. Imagine the possibilities if we could see ourselves the same way God sees us!

Much of the time we are not able to see our purpose and destiny with much clarity, so we are required to rely on faith. The principle of faith allows us to trust that there is something special and unique for us, even if our experiences have been the opposite. Sometimes there is great resistance or even setbacks before we are able to get into the fullness of God's desires for us.

> *Now faith is confidence in what we hope for and assurance about what we do not see* (Hebrews 11:1).

We need to be certain of the fact that God has nothing but good intentions for us, even though we may not see them yet.

> *"For I know the plans I have for you," declares the Lord, "plans to prosper you and not to harm you, plans to give you hope and a future"* (Jeremiah 29:11).

God's intentions for us are to prosper us, to give us hope and a future. If you read on, you'll see the benefits of grasping this truth.

> *Then you will call on me and come and pray to me, and I*
> *will listen to you. You will seek me and find me when you*
> *seek me with all your heart* (Jeremiah 29:12–13).

We must see what God is doing in our lives and work with Him to bring it about. It is time to take a stand against what Satan has in mind for us and come into line with God's wonderful intentions for us.

> *If people can't see what God is doing, they stumble all over*
> *themselves; but when they attend to what he reveals, they*
> *are most blessed* (Proverbs 29:18 The Message).

The King's Table

I had a vision of a long table in Heaven that seemed to stretch for eternity. God the Father, the King, was sitting at the head of the table. Yet, there were only a few people sitting at the table having a close relationship with the King, like family at a dinner table. There were so many empty chairs.

Then I saw people standing at attention like butlers or servants around the outside perimeter of the room, waiting for orders from the King. I knew that the servants had sincere hearts and were saying, "I will do whatever God asks me to do." They were not aware that God was asking them to come to the table for a closer relationship with Him and receive greater authority.

I realized that their theology and belief systems were holding them back. In many cases, God had stopped speaking to some of these servants because He was waiting for them to mature and know His heart, and not have to be told everything they needed to do.

Yes, we all need to be servants. We learn a lot in that stage of maturity. But many are now invited to sit at the table with the King as His sons and daughters. At this stage of maturity, God can turn to us and say, "I want to bless what you want because your heart is in line with Mine" (Psalm 37:4, paraphrased).

Activation Prayer to Receive Your Invitation

God, your true and eternal Father, is inviting you as a son or a daughter to sit at His table and enjoy a time of close relationship with Him. As I saw in the vision, most of us do not realize that the invitation is to everyone, not just the more mature in Christ. Family means all ages are invited!

> *Jesus said, "Let the little children come to me, and do not hinder them, for the kingdom of heaven belongs to such as these"* (Matthew 19:14).

You do not have to wait until you get to Heaven. You can do this now. I want to help you, so I have written the following prayer for you to read out loud and from your heart:

> *Heavenly Father, great King at the table, I gladly accept Your invitation to become Your child. Father, I thank You for training me to serve You, and ask that You continue to teach me. I gladly take the seat with my name on it—that seat of greater authority and deeper intimacy with You. God, I accept my place in the Kingdom family business. Help me demonstrate Your love and power on earth. Amen.*

Your Father's Voice

> *For God does speak—now one way, now another—though no one perceives it* (Job 33:14).

Most Christians believe that God still speaks to people today, just not necessarily to them. If we continually focus on not being able to do something, chances are we never will. But if we change our focus and accept that God loves us and longs to speak to us, we will begin to hear God in ways we never thought possible.

Sometimes God speaks more dramatically through divine circumstances, and you know without a doubt it was Him. I have had many dramatic encounters over the years. For instance, I once saw an angel standing at the foot of my bed. Another time, an ancient parchment literally appeared in midair. I have been taken in the spirit to a church that I was going to visit the next day, and I have even seen into Heaven. But most of the time, revelation comes in the form of a small, quiet voice inside.

God longs to convey messages of love, comfort, guidance, and warning through a variety of methods. These messages may come through dreams and visions, reading the Bible, a conversation, or through nature, music, and the arts. The possibilities are endless!

Anyone can learn to discern what is happening in the atmosphere around them and to recognize God's voice. I wrote this book to help you sharpen your spiritual discernment.

Five Potential Roadblocks to Hearing God

Therefore, since we are surrounded by such a great cloud of witnesses, let us throw off everything that hinders (Hebrews 12:1).

Let's face it, the phrase "hearing God" has some baggage. Due to some immature prophetic people, many have been wounded during their journey toward hearing God. My experience is that most Christians have not been trained on how to develop a relationship with God, how to respond to Him, or to understand His timing. But we must not throw out the baby with the bathwater! God still speaks today, and hearing His voice for yourself will activate you into a deeper relationship with Him.

Since our beliefs are formed at an early age, we all can carry around some "belief baggage" that is not necessarily based on fact or reality. In many cases, strongly held beliefs that have been passed down through generations are not actually based on the Bible. Some beliefs have been based on a Bible verse, but were taken out of context and have not been understood the way they were originally intended.

Jesus often said the words "believe and you will receive." We need to examine what we believe, because negativity and criticism are like dark filters that distort how we view God, others, and ourselves.

The following are five potential roadblocks you might be facing, or may face in the future, as you learn to hear God.

1. Misconception

Just after Jesus taught the disciples to pray the Lord's Prayer (Luke 11), He told two parables to activate it. One was of a man who needed bread in the middle of the night, so he came to a friend's house and persisted in asking until he got it:

> *I tell you, even though he will not get up and give you the bread because of friendship, yet **because of your shameless audacity he will surely get up and give you as much as you need.** So I say to you: **Ask** and it will be given to you; **seek** and you will find; **knock** and the door will be opened to you. For everyone who asks receives; the one who seeks finds; and to the one who knocks, the door will be opened* (Luke 11:8–10).

We need to "ask," "seek," and "knock," and have "shameless audacity!"

Then Jesus goes right into another parable that explains God's heart as a father. This provides confidence and trust that God will speak to us.

> *Which of you fathers, if your son asks for a fish, will give him a snake instead? Or if he asks for an egg, will give him a scorpion? If you then, though you are evil, know how to give good gifts to your children, how much more will your Father in heaven give the Holy Spirit to those who ask him!* (Luke 11:11–13)

If we have a preconceived belief that God is harsh or militant, we will interpret the things He says to us through a filter of fear. But God is a good, loving Father who gives good gifts to His children. Go beyond believing that God wants to speak to you, and know that you can get bold and trust God to answer you. If you already hear Him— ask for more.

2. Fear

> *For God has not given us a spirit of fear, but of power and of love and of a sound mind* (2 Timothy 1:7 NKJV).

Many people are afraid that they will be deceived or that what they are asking is not in God's will. Trust God as a Father. Your heavenly Father does not want to be harsh or mean to you. If you are trying to be perfect, there is no room for you to grow. God uses our mistakes to train us. I have made my share of mistakes—and I still do—but God uses them to teach me and help me make a greater impact later.

Fear of being judged and rejected by others has caused an overemphasis on 100 percent accuracy. Too many people have decided that "If it is not 100 percent God, then I am not saying anything," because of painful repercussions from well-meaning church leaders. This shuts us down from maturing in hearing God. It is possible to become more accurate over time, but it really does take practice. If you are not sharing with others what you see and hear, then you are not practicing. See the dilemma?

It is important to understand that we will never be 100 percent accurate. There are times when *we know in part and we prophesy in part* (1 Corinthians 13:9), not knowing the full message. God says that we are to love each other. One of the ways He helps us do that is by making us need each other. He often gives people different parts of a message, like puzzle pieces, so that we have to bring our pieces together before we can see the whole picture. When we practice hearing God together, we grow closer to Him and to one another!

3. Logic and Reasoning

> *Now faith is confidence in what we hope for and assurance about what we do not see* (Hebrews 11:1).

Most of us were raised with a logical mindset based in the scientific method, which depends on being able to get the same results in exactly the same way, time after time. But God likes to change things up! For example, Jesus healed blindness at least three different ways: He spit on a guy's eyes (Mark 8:23), He cast out a demon (Matthew 12:22), and He told blind Bartimaeus that his own faith had made him well (Mark 10:52).

Bartimaeus is a prime example that faith is being sure of what we do *not* see. God's supernatural power through the Holy Spirit is far beyond logic. We must be careful not to get into a "show me the money" mentality.

4. Not Knowing How to Respond

Even when we do hear God clearly, often how we respond to what we are hearing can be a hindrance. We need to be careful not to assume that we understand what He is saying today just because we have heard it before.

Here is a good example from the Bible: God spoke to Peter in a vision to do something that was against his beliefs—to eat animals that were considered unclean by the Jewish Law. God was not speaking to Peter about changing his diet, but about his need to make a theological and relational change that would consider all people equal. Peter had to respond and went to the house of Cornelius, a Gentile, and everyone in his house was filled with the Holy Spirit. This brought about a major change in perspective for the early Church.

5. Time with God

> But Jesus often withdrew to lonely places and prayed (Luke 5:16).

It helps to realize that you will go through times when you have more or less time with God, depending on your life situation. A key is to think in terms of having a relationship with a living Person. God longs for us to commune with Him like a father would with his children. What if your child said to you, "I love you, but I really do not want to spend time with you." We can love God, but we need to seek a personal relationship so we know His heart and ways, and understand that He wants nothing but the best for us.

Ever notice that you tend to hear God or get big ideas while in the shower, driving, or simply taking a walk? These are just a few of the places and times when we naturally calm down and listen. Notice that in all of these situations we are usually alone and doing something routine. Because we want to develop a real relationship with God, we can check in with Him throughout the day, no matter what we are doing or what need may arise.

However, in order to have a strong and deep relationship with anybody, it really is important to set aside some "us time." We all need to have quiet, one-on-one time with the people most important to us. Simply being together and not saying much of anything can sometimes be as profound and unifying as having deep and meaningful conversations. Our relationship with God needs "us time" as much as any other!

It is good to set time aside regularly—daily, if possible—to quiet yourself. It does not matter when or how long—just do it!

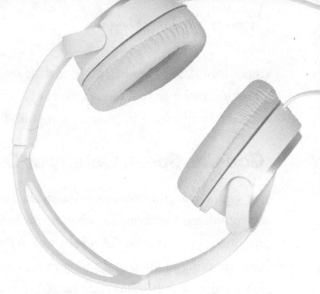

CHAPTER 2

Recognizing God's Voice ～

Now faith is confidence in what we hope for and assurance about what we do not see (Hebrews 11:1).

To start recognizing the voice of God, we need to move out of our comfort zone of logic and reasoning. Most people have a "prove it to me" mentality because they were raised and trained to think logically. But faith is being sure of what we do *not* see! God's supernatural power through the Holy Spirit is far beyond scientific logic and reasoning.

For example, my DNA shows that I have Huntington's disease, but I was supernaturally healed of the symptoms. Medically speaking, I should be sick. Yet my body and mind have been fine since 2001. That is not logical, but I am healed. In fact, at age fifty-nine as I am writing this, the Huntington's Disease Center of Excellence at UCLA has asked to place me in a study because my symptom-free life is unheard of!

God Can Speak Quietly or Dramatically

Unless we train ourselves to watch and listen, many experiences can be considered a coincidence when it was really God trying to get our attention. I was once awakened at three in the morning by the voice of God speaking so softly and subtly that I could have missed it. Then I felt a spiritual shift occur and realized that an angel was in my room, even though I did not see anything. I recognized what was happening because I have trained myself to discern and have put into practice what I have learned. You can learn to sharpen your spiritual discernment, just like I have.

Now let me share a story with you in which God spoke more dramatically. Keep in mind that it really does not matter how dramatically God speaks; it is all from Him and is designed to get us to take action in our lives.

Though I currently live in Los Angeles, a few years ago, I moved to Santa Maria, California. I knew God had called me and I received lots of confirmation, but I really needed to hear His plan and strategy for being there. I cried out to God daily on my prayer walks asking for this.

The pastor of a church in Apopka, Florida, had seen me do "rapid-fire prophecy" in the past when we were doing activations prior to a prophetic outreach. He invited me to come and prophesy over his entire church. There were more than 500 people, and I knew that I could do about 100 an hour, so we lined up four meetings; and by lunchtime on Sunday, I had successfully prophesied over his entire church.

I flew back to California, physically exhausted from a weekend full of prophesying, and finally fell into bed after midnight. I knew that

I was about to receive revelation because I freely gave out so much. It is a principle of God's Kingdom that the more you give, the more you receive. So, I was spiritually "full" and ready to receive.

I woke up in the middle of the night to a golden man standing at the foot of my bed. I knew it was an angel. The presence of God was so strong in my room as the angel stood, not saying a word. But I was extremely tired, so I sat up in bed and asked, "Can you give me what you are going to tell me in a dream?"

I fell back on my pillow and was instantly in a dream with the angel standing next to me. He took me to three places in Santa Maria, where I lived, and showed me things in each one that I had never seen in the natural realm. The next day my wife and I drove to these places, and recognized exactly what I had seen in the dream. I could see why God had moved us there and better understood what He wanted me to do. This was definitely a dramatic encounter, but what really matters is that God is speaking and you can learn to discern His voice.

Learning more information and gaining more knowledge only helps when you practice the things that you have learned. I want to help you know that God is real in your life. I practice hearing God daily—yes, every day—as if I were a well-prepared athlete training for a sport. Over time, recognizing God's voice will become supernaturally natural for you.

Practical Tips to Recognize God's Voice

Keep in mind that you do not need to have a dramatic encounter to hear the voice of God. You don't have to have an angel stand in front of you or a visitation from Jesus. In fact, these things may happen on occasion but they are very rare. What matters more is to develop your relationship with God as the Father and Jesus as the Lord of your life. God speaks in many different ways and even for me, a seasoned and experienced prophetic minister, I still hear God's still, small voice through the Holy Spirit each and every day!

I want to share with you some very practical things that you can do where you are right now. Whether you are new at hearing God or a veteran, these are things that we all need to keep in mind. When I find that God seems to stop speaking to me, I go back and check some of these areas in my life.

Believe That God Wants to Speak to You

> *Jesus replied, "Blessed are you, Simon son of Jonah, for this was not revealed to you by flesh and blood, but by my Father in heaven"* (Matthew 16:17).

A widespread misunderstanding is that God only speaks to people who have been to Bible college and are ordained ministers. But the example in Matthew 16:17 shows that Peter, an uneducated, blue-collar business owner, heard directly from God. A roadblock to hearing God that many people face is the belief that God still speaks to *some* people today, just not them.

I said this in the first chapter, but it bears repeating: If we continually focus on not being able to do something, chances are we never will. We can change our focus and accept that God longs to speak to us! Once we do, we will begin to hear God in ways we never imagined. Get bold and ask God to speak to you. If you already hear Him, ask for more!

Persistence Pays

> *So I say to you: Ask and it will be given to you; seek and you will find; knock and the door will be opened to you. For everyone who asks receives; the one who seeks*

finds; and to the one who knocks, the door will be opened
(Luke 11:9–10).

You must move beyond hoping that God wants to speak to you
and *know* that you can get bold and trust God to answer you. Many
people are afraid that they will be deceived or that what they are asking
is not in God's will. Your heavenly Father does not want to be harsh or
mean to you. God is a good and loving Father who gives good gifts to
His children.

Track What You Hear from God

Quite often God speaks over time. Most people miss this process
because they do not track what they hear. In my opinion, hearing God
clearly cannot be done without valuing what He is speaking to you and
tracking it over time. Since I take time to journal every day, I am continually surprised to see things come to pass that God had spoken to me
previously. Daily journaling is my number one way to learn to discern.

Respond to What God Says to You

*But the one who hears my words and does not put them
into practice is like a man who built a house on the ground
without a foundation* (Luke 6:49).

I had a dream about my best friend from high school, whom I have
not seen in more than thirty years. In the dream, he was going through a
difficult time. I responded by praying for him even though I had no idea
what was happening with him and had no way of contacting him. I have
learned that, as God reveals things to you, responding in faith will activate you to receive even more. Praying is always the best first response!

As another example, a few years ago I heard God say that the "Joseph
Anointing" is coming. I knew that this was based on Genesis 40–41,
where Joseph interpreted Pharaoh's dreams and gave the leader

prophetic wisdom on how to respond. Joseph's response changed the course of history!

I did not want to assume that I understood what God meant, so that same morning I bought a book by Johnny Enlow, *The Seven Mountain Mantle: Receiving the Joseph Anointing to Reform Nations*. Not only had Johnny and I received revelation about the subject at the same time, he had some amazing insight that really helped my life. We met two years later and have become friends. We even minister together on occasion.

You Will Need to Practice

> *But solid food is for the mature, who by constant use have trained themselves to distinguish good from evil* (Hebrews 5:14).

God wants to interact with you regularly; however, to hear God consistently and accurately takes practice. For instance, ask God what the next song will be when you listen to the radio. Pay attention to how the answer comes to you: maybe a brief thought, a mental picture, or hearing a few lines of the song before it was played. Then notice the difference when you heard right compared to when you missed it.

You can ask God who is calling you on the phone before you look at your caller ID. When you feel like you need to take something with you on a trip, but it doesn't make sense, take it along anyway and see what happens. When you cannot find something, ask the Holy Spirit to show you where it is.

Developing Your Spiritual Eyes

It is important to recognize the source of what you are perceiving spiritually—is it yourself, from God, or other sources? Remember, we need to *learn* to discern God's voice. So, activate your faith by taking notes and practicing what you learn along the way. We are going to explore our spiritual senses, particularly having *"eyes to see"* and *"ears to hear."* When it comes to learning to discern and hearing God, most people think that you should just listen to God speak internally to your spirit, like words in your mind, and then share word-for-word what you are hearing. This is having *"ears to hear,"* but it is only one way that God speaks. We also must learn to develop other "spiritual senses," through the Holy Spirit.

Eyes to See

Throughout the Bible, God shows us various ways that He speaks symbolically through prophecy, dreams, visions, supernatural encounters, and prophetic life parables. Jesus told us that we must have eyes that can see and ears that can hear. But most people only see with their natural eyes because we are trained from an early age to think logically and not value our imagination.

God often speaks using symbolic language, such as metaphors, rhymes, and wordplay. Consider God's conversation with the prophet Jeremiah:

> *The word of the Lord came to me: "What do you see, Jeremiah?" "I see the branch of an almond tree," I replied. The Lord said to me, "You have seen correctly, for I am watching to see that my word is fulfilled"* (Jeremiah 1:11–12).

God asked Jeremiah what he could see, not what he could hear. It is interesting to note that the Hebrew word for "watching" *(shaqad)* sounds similar to the Hebrew word for "almond tree" *(shaqed)*. A modern-day example of God speaking this way might be you seeing a pickup truck, and God saying that things are about to "pick up" for you.

God spoke similarly to the prophet Amos:

> *This is what the Sovereign Lord showed me: a basket of ripe fruit. "What do you see, Amos?" he asked. "A basket of ripe fruit," I answered. Then the Lord said to me, "The time is ripe for my people Israel ..."* (Amos 8:1–2).

Through these examples, we see that God can be much more creative when communicating with us than we've been taught!

Eye-Opening Experiences

It is interesting that Jesus chose the words *"eyes to see"* because we read early in the Bible that our spiritual eyes have been a target of Satan from the very beginning:

> *The woman said to the serpent, "We may eat fruit from the trees in the garden, but God did say, 'You must not eat fruit from the tree that is in the middle of the garden, and you must not touch it, or you will die.'"*
>
> *"You will not certainly die," the serpent said to the woman. "For God knows that when you eat from it **your eyes will be opened,** and you will be like God, knowing good and evil"* (Genesis 3:2–5).

Satan told Eve that her eyes would be opened if she ate from the Tree of the Knowledge of Good and Evil. But Satan is a liar! Their eyes were not opened; instead, they were closed to the spiritual realm:

> *The god of this age has blinded the minds of unbelievers, so that they cannot see the light of the gospel that displays the glory of Christ, who is the image of God* (2 Corinthians 4:4).

This actually is a good description of people who do not believe that God speaks today. Like Eve, they have believed a lie and have become spiritually blind. If you have ever received Jesus or had a born-again or radical experience with God, it happened because God gave you a "revelation of Him." God reveals Himself to people and draws them close through the Spirit of prophecy, the Holy Spirit: *"For it is the Spirit of prophecy who bears testimony to Jesus"* (Revelation 19:10).

In Acts 9, Jesus appeared to Saul (later named Paul) in a vision that blinded him for three days. That was radical, but Paul had a radical calling. In Acts 26, Paul tells more about that encounter with Jesus on the road that day. Speaking to Paul, Jesus said:

> *I will rescue you from your own people and from the Gentiles. I am sending you to them to **open their eyes** and turn them from darkness to light, and from the power of Satan to God, so that they may receive forgiveness of sins and a place among those who are sanctified by faith in me"* (Acts 26:17–18).

A primary work of God in our lives is restoring our *"eyes to see"* and healing us from the spiritual blindness humans have been afflicted with since the beginning. I believe you will find that He really is interested and wants to be involved in even the least world-changing matters of your life!

God's Will and Timing

An important aspect of responding to what God is speaking to you is understanding His will and timing. There are several variables you have to take into consideration, and it is not always easy. You may find yourself going through one of the following seasons or situations:

1. You are in the process of learning life lessons. It seems like God is holding you back, but He is actually training you. This is the wilderness where nothing seems to work because God is working things out *in* you. Your spiritual life feels dry, and it is hard to hear God's voice. Do not strive or try to force things to happen. God may be working on patience, love, and humility in your life.

2. Nothing seems to be happening because *God is waiting on you* **to move forward.** If all the pieces are there, but God is silent, you need to do the last thing you heard. This happened to me a few years ago. When I remembered that God had called me to launch my internet training—and I did it—things began to move and I could hear God again.

3. Spiritual warfare holds you back. When it feels like you are going against the wind, then "something" does not want you to move forward. The remedy is to agree with others in prayer and break through whatever is resisting God's will for you.

4. The "Job Syndrome." If you are going through a season of collapse, you may be in a time that is similar to the book of Job. Everything was stripped from Job. God allows us to endure hardship and loss so He can pay us back double. Do not give up. Trust God.

5. Recent spiritual promotion. You now have to walk through resistance from the enemy. David was anointed by Samuel to be the next king of Israel, only to be chased by Saul, the currently reigning king. Moses had face-to-face encounters with God, but the people would not listen to him. Paul had a radical encounter with Jesus, but was continually resisted by his former friends and colleagues.

From 2008 through 2013, I went through a serious Job Syndrome time. God told me in advance, but it was still a terrible five years. I lost favor and was banned from speaking in churches I helped start. People lied about me and misunderstood me. I got really sick, my family members got sick, and some of them died. I lost my vision, all my outreach teams and my staff. These are just a few of the things that happened during that time.

But, in the midst of it, I had some amazing angelic encounters that I will talk about in Chapter 12. God used that time to test and prepare me for what I am doing now. It ended with a visitation from Jesus.

Knowing Your Season

The "dark night of the soul" is a term made popular by Saint John of the Cross in the sixteenth century. It is just another way of describing the wilderness, or a time when things are not clear and God is working on things in us. At the same time, the enemy will test us. Even Jesus went through this before He began public ministry.

Even so, I think that Christians today put too much emphasis on it. Because I spent so much time in the dark night of the soul, I developed the training you are going through in this book. After years of my own experiences and working with people, I have found it is much more beneficial to focus on the *bright day of the Spirit!*

Most people confuse a wilderness time with a Job season. Others even try to make it happen in their own strength by not working and selling everything. I have met lots of people who said they want to lose everything so they can gain double. They believe they are trusting God, but they are actually trying to artificially gain a promotion. This is false humility and evidence of a misguided belief system. If a Job season does come to you, it will be later in your spiritual life, just before a promotion, and is not always necessary.

You can stay out of the wilderness, (or shorten your time there) by recognizing the lesson that God wants you to learn and responding appropriately. If you have been in a difficult time for a while, ask God to show you what the root is and get an exit strategy! If there seems to be a set time for you, like Jesus' forty days in the desert, then make the most of it by journaling your insights and allowing God to draw you close. Focus on Him and you will emerge from the wilderness leaning on God like never before! (See Song of Solomon 8:5.)

CHAPTER 3

Perceiving the Source

Tuning In to God

Some people know all their lives that they have had a special ability to perceive spiritual things, but do not realize they are picking up on a source other than God's Holy Spirit. They will sometimes describe their experiences as a "sixth sense" or a subtle "knowing" that they cannot explain. These people have a true gift from God, but do not realize how to point it in the right direction to truly hear God.

Like the tuner on a car radio, you have to choose a certain frequency to get the station you want to hear. Sometimes the stations can be so close in frequency that you can hear parts of both at the same time, or the signal will switch back and forth between the two. In a similar way, people can "pick up" spiritual signals and not be aware that they need to be intentional about what "station" they want to tune in to.

Because they are not always hearing from God, psychics and untrained Christians can tap into the soulish and demonic realms, and tell you things that already exist, as though they have not happened yet. Then, when it happens, you believe the person had heard from God and the person gains credibility with you.

How I Learned This Lesson

That happened to me years ago. A woman in my church was operating in a "mixture of the soul and the spirit" because of her immaturity. She told me, "So that you will know I am a prophetess sent to you from God, you are going to receive a $10,000 check in the mail this week. The Lord is telling you to quit your job because there will be more checks coming to you." Sure enough I received the check the next day, but I did not realize that it had been mailed a week before. A demonic force was trying to pass this "information" off as if it was revelation from God.

The Bible tells us to test prophetic words and weigh them carefully (1 Corinthians 14:29). Yes, I got the first check but the other checks never followed. Had I listened to this woman's prophetic word to me to quit my job, I would have gone into financial ruin. Also notice that the prophetic word she gave is giving praise to her as a prophetess and not to the Lord. You will grow in your ability to discern what is not from God if you apply what I am teaching you in this book to your own life experiences. Have no fear!

Spirit Versus Soul

For in him [Jesus] all things were created: things in heaven and on earth, visible and invisible, whether thrones or powers or rulers or authorities; all things have been created by him and for him (Colossians 1:16).

A common theme in the Bible is the conflict between the soul and the spirit. The Greek word for "soul" is *psuche* (where we get the word "psychic") and the Greek for "spirit" is *pneuma*. Like spiritual blindness, two different sources of revelation have their roots in the very beginning of the Bible.

In Genesis 2, there were two trees in the Garden of Eden: the Tree of Life and the Tree of the Knowledge of Good and Evil. As the name implies, the Tree of Life *gave life* and represented the Spirit of God *(pneuma)*. The Tree of the Knowledge of Good and Evil ultimately *took life* and represented the soulish realm of Satan *(psuche)*. God told Adam and Eve not to eat from the Tree of the Knowledge of Good and Evil, or they would die.

God is the Creator of everything, and the Giver of all good things. Spiritual gifts are from God, not Satan or anyone else. The Hebrew word for "create," *barah,* means "something out of nothing," and is used only in reference to God and His activity. Because Satan cannot create, he can only distort and counterfeit the gifts that come from God.

People can have spiritual gifts from God that were given at their birth. For instance, the prophet Jeremiah was gifted as a prophet while still in his mother's womb (Jeremiah 1:5). David realized that his destiny in God emerged while he was still an infant (Psalm 22:9–10). Timothy, on the other hand, received his gifts as the apostle Paul laid his hands on him and prayed (2 Timothy 1:6).

These gifts belong to us apart from any spiritual understanding or manner of religious upbringing. The most important thing is what we choose to do with them.

Some so-called psychics are outright fakes with no spiritual gift at all, but have learned to deceive and manipulate people for their own gain. Since I have learned to discern, I train others how to discern the genuine voice of God from other sources. Most people simply do not understand that there is a difference.

Dispelling the "Fear to Hear"

> *For God has not given us a spirit of fear, but of power and of love and of a sound mind* (2 Timothy 1:7 NKJV).

The phrase *"do not be afraid"* appears in the Bible nearly seventy times. That is a lot! Getting eyes to see involves clearing away doubt and unbelief from our spiritual lenses, along with critical and judgmental attitudes. These have led to spiritual dullness and have stolen our ability to discern what God is saying and doing today. Because we have lost the ability to discern, many people are fearful of being deceived. But fear is actually a negative spirit that clouds vision and misdirects focus.

As we explored in Chapters 1 and 2, God is the good Father, eager to share with His children what is on His heart and mind. He is endlessly creative in how He communicates to us. Learning to discern what He is saying is meant to be a joyful process, not one to fear! Hebrews 4:16 says: *"Let us then approach God's throne of grace with confidence, so that we may receive mercy and find grace to help us in our time of need."* One of our greatest *needs* is hearing God's voice, so we can be confident He will extend us mercy and grace as we grow in this.

Fear of Being Deceived

As you step out more and develop your ability to hear the voice of God, you will encounter both positive and negative words. Most negative words of knowledge and prophecy come from discerning the enemy's will for the person instead of God's will.

The purpose of hearing God is to destroy the works of Satan. So whenever you see the destruction of Satan in a person's life, you can choose to flip it—and flip it good! *"'For I know the plans I have for you,' declares the Lord, 'plans to prosper you and not to harm you, plans to give you hope and a future'"* (Jeremiah 29:11). God's plans for people are *always* good!

In a later chapter, I will go into more detail about how to flip a negative word or situation. This is a big key to effectively hearing God. We need to learn how to respond to negative things and bring God's redemptive value to them. I write about this a lot, and you may think I am repeating myself at times, but this is one thing that will help you the most. Unfortunately, it is probably opposite of what you have been taught!

Fear of Being Wrong

When it comes to hearing God, there has been an unhealthy emphasis on perfect accuracy. Many people think, *If I'm not 100 percent certain it's from God, then I'm not saying anything.* This is a legalistic view of how God speaks, and it does not reveal God's heart of grace. This fear shuts us down from maturing in hearing God. It is possible to hear God with increasing clarity, but it takes practice and is a process.

If you are not sharing what you perceive with others, then you are not practicing. See the dilemma? We will never be 100 percent accurate because we *"know in part and we prophesy in part,"* not seeing the full picture or knowing the full message (1 Corinthians 13:9). If you strive for perfection, there is no room for growth. God uses our mistakes to train us. I have made my share of mistakes, and I still do. In His grace, God uses them to help me make a greater impact later.

You may ask, "Then what should I do when it turns out I was wrong?" Humility is the key. Own up to your mistake and admit that you are still learning how to hear and sense God more clearly.

Know also that you might not even be technically "wrong," but simply picked up on something for later and it will not be evident until the time comes. Or, in other cases, the person does not immediately make the connection and only realizes later—maybe much later—that what you shared was important and helpful.

Fear of Disappointing God

> *Jesus said, "Let the little children come to me, and do not hinder them, for the kingdom of heaven belongs to such as these"* (Matthew 19:14).

Remember the vision of the King's table I shared in the first chapter? One of the main things God spoke to me through that vision was that His table is open to everyone, not just the more mature in Christ. Too often we assume it takes man's approval to be part of the "family of God"—but family means all ages are invited.

God does not hate or reject immaturity. He sees you as who you will become, even while you still have a long development process ahead of you. God is not impatient with immaturity—He *enjoys* relating to you as you grow. You would never expect a five-year-old to drive a car! In the same way, God does not expect more from you than your current level of maturity allows. As you grow and mature, God will test you with the purpose of promoting you into greater levels of influence and maturity.

For example, I used to focus on demons and spent a lot of time and energy discerning what the enemy was doing. Later, I realized that while it is useful for some situations, our main focus should be on what *God* is doing. This is how we receive the promotions, opportunities, and other good things He wants to bring to us and through us.

So go ahead and put on your Holy Spirit training wheels. It is okay to practice and to make mistakes. That is the only way to learn! If you do not have a lot of experience, you may not want to start by sharing something in front of a group. Instead, start out by gathering a few people you know and trust. Strong, nurturing relationships create a safe environment to practice without fear. Let them know you are practicing, and even invite them to practice with you. I have trained a lot of people to use the line, "I am taking a class on hearing God and how to encourage people. Can I practice on you?" Just know that God loves you, has grace for you and wants to speak to you. Remember, learning is a process.

Fear of Being Judged and Rejected

> *Yet at the same time many even among the leaders believed in him. But because of the Pharisees they would not openly acknowledge their faith for fear they would be put out of the synagogue* (John 12:42).

If we stay grounded on what God says biblically and constantly use our gifts, we will not have to worry about being deceived, being wrong, disappointing God, or fearing rejection.

Study the Real to Spot the Counterfeit

In Revelation 3:18, Jesus told the Church of Laodicea they were lukewarm toward Him, and they had lost the ability to see and hear. His remedy for their blindness was, *"buy from me ... salve to put on your eyes, so you can see."*

You have to become so in touch with the real voice of God that you can easily recognize other sources. If you went to work for a bank in the counterfeit money department, your training would be focused on how real money looks and feels. By knowing and understanding the real, detecting counterfeit currency becomes easier. So, do not focus on counterfeit voices; focus on God's!

One of the biggest pitfalls Christians face when learning to hear God is focusing on the enemy and demons rather than God and angels. We can get preoccupied with what is wrong with ourselves and others and miss the opportunity to build each other up and celebrate the fact that we are God's children.

Discerning God's voice comes with practice. What you perceive needs to be in harmony with biblical principles. Even if it offends you, it might be from God because He is trying to change your thinking. Remember how Peter was offended with what God said to him in Acts 10 about eating unclean animals? God will often stretch us and ask us to go outside our comfort zones. But when you pray about it, you will usually get confirmations and you will know it is Him by a sense of peace and absence of fear.

Testing, Judging, and Researching a Prophetic Word

The best way to test a prophetic word is to begin by writing it down. Ask God to reveal to you if it is from Him, to remind you if He has spoken something similar to you before, and to show you whether it lines up with His written Word, the Bible. Also, consider whether you know the person who gave you the word, and if there is positive fruit in his or her life. Did the spirit behind it feel positive or negative? If God confirms the word to you in some way, ask Him about the timing: is it for now or later?

There are clues to help you recognize whether you are judging a word critically or honestly examining it to see if it is from God. For example, do you quickly assume it is wrong before even considering that it could be right? Maybe you begin to doubt that the person is hearing God, or that God is speaking to you. Did you write it down and pray about it first?

Many people do not know the difference between testing a word to see if there is any good in it, as opposed to judging it with a critical spirit. This comes by practice.

> *Solid food is for the mature, who by constant use have trained themselves to distinguish good from evil* (Hebrews 5:14).

It can sound wise and discerning to say, "Where's that in the Bible?" But did you ask God to show you and search the biblical principles out for yourself? It can be easy to assume that if a word does not come about, then the person must be a false prophet. However, as we will discover, inaccuracy is not the sign of a false prophet.

Prophetic words can be especially tricky and complicated since other people are often involved. Take the topic of marriage partners, for example. If you feel like God is telling you that you are going to marry a certain person, you need to get more than one word and will need lots of confirmations. Too often, marriage words we receive on our own from God can be clouded with our own desires. On the other hand, it could indeed be God's will or desire, but if the other person says no, then it will not happen. God never forces Himself on anyone, so if you heard God say to marry someone, you need to hold that loosely.

Many people have shipwrecked themselves on the rocks of prophetic disappointment that sent them spinning away from their true love—God. If this is you, or someone you know, let it go and ask God to bring His perfect plan for you. Ask God to open your eyes to the life lessons He is trying to teach you through the hard time. Remember that God wants to be your true love. Do not let disappointments from prophetic words separate you from Him.

Prayers to Activate Faith and Spiritual Senses

The following is a great Bible verse to pray over yourself and those you love:

> *I pray that the eyes of your heart may be enlightened in order that you may know the hope to which he has called you, the riches of his glorious inheritance in his holy people and his incomparably great power for us who believe* (Ephesians 1:18–19).

The starting place for reversing spiritual dullness is focusing our attention back on the supernatural things of God. Dullness will quickly be wiped away and our focus will sharpen into greater spiritual awareness.

The time is ripe to go deeper with God and hear His voice 365 days a year!

> *God, give us eyes to see and ears to hear. Break any negative connections we might have that clouded and blocked our ability to perceive what you are doing. Forgive us if we have not valued words from you or tested them properly. Let us overflow and have an abundance of revelation. In Jesus' name, amen.*

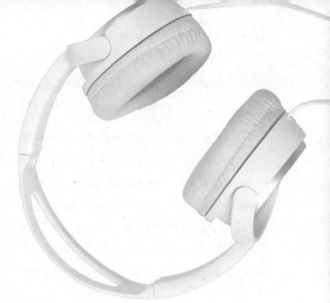

CHAPTER 4

Prophecy and More ⌁

God's Hidden Language

I know it sounds mystical and even exclusive, but God truly does have a special language to communicate the deeper things of His Kingdom.

> The disciples came to him and asked, "Why do you speak to the people in parables?"
>
> He replied, "**Because the knowledge of the secrets of the kingdom of heaven has been given to you, but not to them.** Whoever has will be given more, and they will have an abundance. Whoever does not have, even what they have will be taken from them. This is why I speak to them in

parables: 'Though seeing, they do not see; though hearing, they do not hear or understand'" (Matthew 13:10–13).

In His answer, Jesus addresses the fact that we need to develop our Holy Spirit interpretive ability. The prophet Daniel is a great example of someone with advanced skills in this area: *"because Daniel … was found to have a keen mind and knowledge and understanding, and also the ability to interpret dreams, explain riddles and solve difficult problems"* (Daniel 5:12). Daniel understood God's hidden language, not only in dreams but also in riddles, mysteries, and life parables. I have always had dreams, but my revelation was a trickle compared to what I get now. When I started taking the practical steps I will be showing you, things exploded for me.

It Is God's Nature to Conceal Things

God will hide certain things from those who do not have a relationship with Him because many of the spiritual principles in the Bible work no matter who uses them, for example, "give and you will receive," "what you sow is what you reap," etc.

Today people are discovering these principles without a relationship with God. This is the case with many people in the New Age and Human Potential Movement and people using the Law of Attraction. Yes, the principles work, but they are much more powerful and fulfilling when we apply them in the context of a relationship with God and the empowerment of the Holy Spirit.

Another reason God hides or conceals things is to build a greater desire in you to spend time in His Word and search out truths together with Him. It makes your spiritual journey fun and fulfilling, especially when you find mysteries and secrets of the Kingdom of God.

It is the glory of God to conceal a matter; to search out a matter is the glory of kings (Proverbs 25:2).

It is interesting that Jesus said if we have knowledge of these principles, we will be given more, but whoever does not, even the little bit they have will be taken. This is often the condition of people in churches today, because many have stopped valuing the supernatural side of God in dreams, parables, and spiritual principles. Just as Jesus said, those who have rejected God's hidden ways have had the little they once had taken from them. But Jesus also said that if we value this knowledge (insights hidden in parables and dreams; having eyes to see and ears to hear), we will be given more and will have abundance.

Tips to Gaining Deeper Spiritual Insight

To develop your ability to recognize how God is speaking to you through symbols, start placing value on your dreams and other spiritual insights by writing them down. It also helps to start keeping a daily journal to track what God is saying throughout the day. As you start to accumulate a rich record of your dreams and everyday impressions, you will be able to sift through and mine these experiences for what God is saying.

Read and study the metaphors and symbols in the Bible (parables, dreams, visions, etc.), paying close attention to the ones that are already interpreted for us, like the parable of the seed and soil in Matthew 13.

I also recommend people do daily spiritual activations and exercises, such as going on the internet or social media and considering what other Christians are sensing that God is saying. Take a risk and email or text a prophetic word of encouragement to someone. It is like working out. When you do this consistently, you will be given more revelation than you can imagine. I know, because this is what happened to me!

The Prophetic and Psychic Worlds

I realize that not everyone who reads this book will be in the same place spiritually. Much of what I share with you comes from my own experience of coming out of a dark time in my life, when I was heavily involved in the occult. I had such a radical encounter with Jesus and the Holy Spirit that I have dedicated my life to helping others. For many years, I was a missionary to people in the New Age movement. If you or someone you know is involved in this kind of spirituality, just know I am not judging you. I pray that you, too, will have your own eye-opening experience.

Since I was a young child, I could hear and communicate in the spiritual realm. I had foreknowledge of events and "knew stuff." I had been involved for many years in occult practice, so I heard from sources other than the Holy Spirit. In the late 1970s, God began drawing me to Himself; but when I started going to church, I was told my gifts were of the devil. This was very confusing until I found Spirit-filled Christians who helped me develop and understand my spiritual gifts, and how to use them only for God.

The popularity of psychics today should not discourage or intimidate us. It shows that there is a spiritual hunger in people. Personally, I am saddened that so many Christians choose to no longer demonstrate the prophetic gift to the world. How do I know this? I often give prophetic words from God to people in public. The first thing they usually ask is, "Are you a psychic?" When I tell them that I am a Christian, they often say, "I never knew Christians could hear God!"

They do not ask if I am prophetic, because Christians stopped using the prophetic gift in an encouraging and practical way to let people know what God is saying. Instead, people started using it to tell others they are wrong, expose their sin, and claim that God is not happy with them. This is not the heart of God at all, and it is not prophetic. My goodness, we have our work cut out for us to demonstrate the real heart of God to the world!

I want to be clear that I am not judging you or anyone you might know who goes to psychics or who may be involved in New Age practices. Many people have callings from God, like I had, and got pointed in the wrong direction. Or they have not been trained in the things of God and have experienced rejection. I have met and been friends with many New Age people who are kind and loving. What I am about to share are the details of how the spiritual gifts operate and is not meant to bring judgement on people.

Psychics are not hearing from God, but from what many refer to as the "soulish realm," as I discussed in the previous chapter. Many psychics will tell you they hear from God, but they do not understand that not everything in the spirit realm is good or beneficial. Most are not aware that the messages they receive from "spirit guides" come through a demonic network. They will tell you the tools of divination they use, such as tarot cards, stone crystals or specially marked stones called runes. But their source is not the Holy Spirit—Who is the source of revelation for the Spirit-filled Christian.

Two New Agers in the New Testament

In Acts 8:9–25, Philip had an encounter with a "New Age" man named Simon the sorcerer. People followed Simon because they were amazed at what he could do. Simon most likely did not know he was operating in an occult spirit. However, when Philip came in with the real power of God through the Holy Spirit, even Simon wanted it. Most people judge Simon for wanting to buy it, but he repented.

In Acts 13:6–12, the apostle Paul encountered a Jewish sorcerer and false prophet named Bar-Jesus, who had the attention of a prominent government official. When Paul came with the real power of the Holy Spirit, Bar-Jesus opposed him and was blinded for three days. In one case, Simon the sorcerer repented and wanted the gifts of the Holy

Spirit. In another, Bar-Jesus rejected the Holy Spirit and opposed the work of God.

I found that many New Age people are very loving. They like our "light" and "energy," and are open to God's power. Others are more dark and hostile toward Christians and the Holy Spirit; in most cases, they have been wounded by a bad Christian experience. In a later chapter, I will go into how to reach out and bring healing to people who have been wounded terribly by Christians. We need to have eyes to see who is open to the presence and power of the Holy Spirit and who is not. The prophetic gifts work really great for this!

Keys to Discern the Real from the Fake

Knowing and understanding God's heart for people is the best test for knowing the real from the fake. For instance, God will never turn people against each other, threaten people if they do not obey Him, or expose their deepest secrets in a public way. His purpose is always to build people up, not to tear them down or hurt them.

A properly trained, Spirit-filled Christian can tap into God's revelation and tell you something in your life to get your attention (word of knowledge), and then give a genuine prophetic word or message that will give comfort, encouragement, clarity, and strength. Awareness that God is close and that He cares is a consistent result for the one receiving the word.

The main difference between a word from God and a psychic or soulish word is the source of the revelation. Like a bank teller who handles money all day, unless you see and regularly experience the real thing, you will struggle to identify a counterfeit. Psychics may tell you about the future but because they are not actually hearing God, their information will point you away from God's will. If you feel confused or anxious about any message, it is best to let it go.

Discerning God's messages from demonic sources is easy. Demonic sources will not have the characteristics of God in them, and are the opposite of God's will and ways. They often violate biblical principles and provoke unloving and self-seeking behaviors such as anger and revenge. Demonic words lack humility and sound harsh, angry, critical, and are devoid of love. They inspire hopelessness, anxiety, or a spirit of fear, which is not the same as the fear of God.

Discerning our own thoughts and desires from God's takes time and practice. Apart from God, our thoughts often elevate ourselves, can be legalistic or rule-based, and lack God's grace. Our own ideas will usually come to us once or twice, but there will be no other confirmation. The more important the issue—such as changing jobs or homes, or choosing a marriage partner—the more confirmations we need, and from multiple sources.

We all must study and practice hearing from God for ourselves. I have journaled regularly for many years so that I can review and evaluate what I heard and whether anything good came from it. Recognizing the real voice of God in this way has helped me sharpen my discernment. The more you study, practice, and receive feedback, the more you will know what is real.

"Christian Witchcraft"

Unless you have been trained to discern the Holy Spirit, you can pick up on the soulish realm and not realize it. Most of the time when Christians are doing this, they are operating in logic—their own minds or opinions—instead of God's words. If you hear someone doing this, it will be apparent to you because the person's words will not carry the same impact as words from the Holy Spirit. When I hear one of these, I often call it a "good word" as opposed to a "God word."

Many Christians have spiritual gifts that are immature and undeveloped. Oftentimes, they are carrying wounds and have not been fully healed, which causes them to use their God-given spiritual gifts to pray against or even curse people without knowing it. "Christian witchcraft" happens when a believer—even Spirit-filled—begins crossing over into cursing or judging. They use their own opinions or speak from their own wounds, but think it is God speaking to them.

It is true that God will not remove our gifts, *"for God's gifts and his call are irrevocable"* (Romans 11:29), but we can get off track and begin getting signals from other sources, such as the demonic or our own souls. This happened in the life of Samson, who used his God-given strength for his own gain (Judges 15). The prophet Balaam used his gift for sorcery (Numbers 24). King Saul, although anointed by the prophet Samuel, turned his gifts away from God's purposes and later in life ended up consulting a medium for direction (1 Samuel 28).

As I am telling you this, please do not be afraid that you are operating in the wrong spirit. At the end of this chapter, I have included a prayer for you to break ties with anything you may have been involved with in the past.

Spiritual Discernment

> *Finally, brothers and sisters, whatever is true, whatever is noble, whatever is right, whatever is pure, whatever is lovely, whatever is admirable—if anything is excellent or praiseworthy—think about such things* (Philippians 4:8).

The gift of discerning of spirits is often defined as the ability to pick up on the demonic realm and see demons that are holding people down. Because of this, Christians regularly focus on what is wrong instead of on the goodness of God and what His heart is for people. This is tragic, and sadly, it can be hard to get Christians to stop because it is so ingrained in church culture.

When your eyes open up to the spiritual realm, it is very easy to perceive demonic activity, people's sin, and other bad things around you. After I started following Jesus, for the longest time I was overly focused on the negative things in others and myself. Then God reminded me that He is greater than all the negative things. When I started focusing on the goodness of God, my ability to hear His voice became much more clear, and I was actually able to help people.

Jesus had a great conversation with a Samaritan woman at Jacob's well. She arrived at noon to draw water by herself, even though all the other women went in the morning. That is an obvious sign she was an outcast:

> He said to her, "Go, call your husband, and come back." "I have no husband," she replied. Jesus said to her, "You are right when you say you have no husband. The fact is, you have had five husbands, and the man you now have is not your husband. **What you have just said is quite true**" (John 4:16–18).

Notice how Jesus focused in on the desires of her heart. Her behaviors indicated she wanted a loving, healthy relationship with a man, but was either looking in the wrong places or had been wounded. Jesus demonstrated that a word of knowledge could reveal the desires of a person's heart—not to expose sin, but to express God's love and draw the person toward his or her life purpose. The Samaritan woman went on to lead her entire village to put their faith in Jesus as their Messiah. One word from a loving God may have activated the first evangelist!

I cannot emphasize enough that one of the big setbacks we have with hearing God is focusing too much on what is wrong with a person or situation. When Jesus spoke with the Samaritan woman at the well, He mentioned her relationship problems, but went on to acknowledge that she was honest: *"What you have just said is quite true"* (John 4:18). Jesus called an adulterous woman honest! Like Jesus, if we focus on positive, encouraging words, we will not hurt anyone.

The more you grow in hearing God and giving prophetic words, the more you will know what is from God and what is not. For right now, begin to focus on the positive things God is showing you. For instance, it is better to focus on how to improve your golf swing than on why your golf swing is terrible. How you direct your focus determines your results. So, enjoy the game and see yourself getting better—and you will!

Activation Prayer to Remove Negative Spiritual Connections

Since we brought up the occult, psychics, and things of the soul in this book, I have written a prayer as a guide for those who may have been involved with them like I once was. If someone in your family was involved, you will also need to cut off the generational tie. It is good to clean out anything negative, whether we are aware of it or not. If you have not been involved, then you can help others who have.

Read this prayer out loud and from your heart:

> *Father God, I ask that You would cut off any negative spiritual ties that I may have knowingly or unknowingly been involved with in my life. I ask that You would create a clear connection to the Holy Spirit to help me break off any generational curses or ties to the soul or from psychics, the occult, or anything that would stop me from hearing directly and clearly from You. I pray that You would show me what Satan does not want me to see about this so that I can cut the ties clean.*

Father, I ask You to pull forward any gifts that may have been dormant or cut off as a result of my involvement in negative spiritual activities, or those of my ancestors. I ask You to activate and fan into flame all of the gifts You have imparted into my family line so that I may take them to a new level.

And Father, for the times that I have been involved in fear, being overly focused on my own soul or on the enemy, I cut that off as well. I ask that You would replace that with a new focus on You, Holy Spirit, and the angels who serve You, along with all the resources of Heaven available to me.

Lord, activate my ability to hear Your voice, the ability to operate in the prophetic, and to be an encourager. May it be on earth as it is in Heaven. In Jesus' name, amen.

CHAPTER 5

Hearing God through Dreams

Not all dreams are from God, but once you understand how God speaks, you can get a meaning or positive outcome from almost any dream or vision. Over the past 100 years, the field of psychology has approached the subject of dreaming from a soul-focused perspective. This approach relies heavily on using a list of dream symbols from a book, but most of these "dream dictionaries" are not accurate, especially when the dream is from God. I have come to realize that dreams tend to be spiritual, not psychological. Symbols will vary in meaning from dream to dream, so we cannot rely on symbol lists and books.

Dreams: God's Symbolic Language

When I start talking about God's symbolic language and secrets to understanding our dreams, some Christians get uncomfortable because it sounds "occultish." Listen, Jesus was the one who said it plainly:

> *The disciples came to him and asked, "Why do you speak to the people in parables?" He replied, "Because the knowledge of the secrets of the kingdom of heaven has been given to you, but not to them"* (Matthew 13:10–11).

That sounds exclusive, because it is! These are Jesus' very words to His disciples when they came to Him and asked why He spoke in this mysterious, symbolic language called parables. Today, God is still inviting those who truly desire eyes to see and ears to hear into a deeper understanding of His Kingdom. In reality, there is no shortage of revelation from God, but there *is* a shortage of understanding how God speaks. As a result, people aren't able to fulfill what He is saying.

Notice that it is not the parables themselves that are powerful, but the ability to understand the hidden meanings within: *"Whoever has will be given more, and they will have an abundance. Whoever does not have, even what they have will be taken from them"* (Matthew 13:12).

When we let go of hearing God's voice in His deep, mysterious ways, what we have will be taken from us. Unfortunately, this is the condition of many Christians today. But when we value it and ask God to reveal His voice to us, then we will have an abundance.

God communicates through dreams and visions:

> *For God may speak in one way, or in another, yet man does not perceive it.* **In a dream, in a vision of the night,** *when deep sleep falls upon men, while slumbering on their beds, then* **He opens the ears of men, and seals their instruction.** *In order to turn man from his deed, and conceal pride from man* (Job 33:14–17 NKJV).

Dreams are often messages given in God's hidden language, similar to parables. Sometimes we know what our dreams mean and other times we do not. Fortunately, even if we don't understand a dream or vision, God still "seals our instructions," as Job 33:16 says. Sometimes God will give us a dream or revelation and the meaning or fulfillment of it will be sealed away from our natural minds. But because over one-third of the Bible is made up of dreams and visions, it is important to learn to interpret and understand them the best we can.

The Difference between Dreams and Visions

Both dreams and visions can seem very real, much like watching a movie with characters, multiple locations, plot twists, and plenty of action. They can happen when we are awake (daydreams) or while sleeping (night visions). There are also differences between dreams and visions: dreams are usually symbolic and need to be interpreted, while visions tend to be literal and need little, if any, interpretation.

Sometimes dreams and visions overlap. For instance, you could have a vision while dreaming that relates directly to something happening in life, so no interpretation is needed. In the Bible, Joseph was thinking of divorcing Mary until an angel appeared to him (vision) in a dream and told him not to do it (Matthew 1:19–24).

On the other hand, you could have a symbolic vision or picture while you are awake that needs interpretation, much like a dream. For example, in Jeremiah 1:13–15, the prophet did not understand what the boiling pot symbolized until God gave him the interpretation:

> *The word of the Lord came to me again: "What do you see?" "I see a pot that is boiling," I answered. "It is tilting toward us from the north." The Lord said to me, "From the north disaster will be poured out on all who live in the*

land. I am about to summon all the peoples of the north-ern kingdoms," declares the Lord.

Visions can be seen in the mind or imagination, or outward, like a real-life picture or movie that you see with your eyes. The prophet Zechariah wrote that he had a vision during the night, and saw *"a man mounted on a red horse. He was standing among the myrtle trees in a ravine. Behind him were red, brown and white horses"* (Zechariah 1:8). In the vision, the man went on to explain what the horses represented and God's message for His people at that time.

Even though these examples happened in ancient times, when we study them we can learn to understand many of the ways God still speaks to people today. Whatever way you experience it—literal and requiring little interpretation, or symbolic and requiring a lot of inter-pretation—it will always require developing your ability to *apply* God's message to your life. You should always start with prayer, and then maybe do some research if needed. Finish with an action plan for how to respond.

I have seen both literal dreams and symbolic visions. One time I had a dream in which I saw the actual building we were going to rent for our ministry. In the dream, I knew it was an "L" shape with funky look-ing carpet. When we went to look at a building later that day, it was just like I had seen in the dream, and the man renting it to us said, "I apolo-gize for the funky-looking carpet."

Another time, I had a picture in my mind (a vision) of the exact car I wanted to buy. We went to the car dealership, and there it was! Both of these experiences were literal, and I just needed to show up and respond. Of course, I always recommend that you get confirmation on bigger purchases.

On the other hand, you could have a picture in your mind (vision) of an elephant running through your office, which might be symbolic of a greater impact you will have in your business. Or if you have a dream that the governor is dressed like a clown and comes to your house for coffee with your friends, it might be symbolic that new authority (governor) is coming to your relationships and it will be fun (dressed like a clown). Both of these visions are symbolic.

Instead of getting hung up on the terminology of whether it is a dream or a vision, it is more helpful to recognize if it is symbolic—and needs interpretation—or literal, so you can know what type of action you will need to take. You do not have to see literal, movie-like visions for them to be important. Some people see more real-life images and some do not. It does not make them more mature or special to God.

Overview of Dreams and Visions in the Bible

This is not a thorough study, because the goal of this book is to get you to understand dreams quickly. I encourage you to go back and study on your own all the dreams and visions that are in the Bible; there are over 250 references in the Bible—nearly one-third of the Bible. God even used dreams to save the life of the baby Jesus (Matthew 2).

Two major instances of dream interpretation in the Old Testament involve Joseph and Daniel. The butler and the baker and Pharaoh all had dreams that were interpreted by Joseph (read Genesis 40–41). In the second chapter of the book of Daniel, Daniel interpreted King Nebuchadnezzar's dream. In fact, Daniel received the interpretation in a vision. In both Joseph and Daniel's cases, dream interpretation impacted major world leaders and changed the course of history. The common interpretative methods used by the "magicians and wise men" of that day could not interpret these dreams from God. This is still the same today—only God provides or guides dream interpretation. Joseph replied correctly to Pharaoh, "Not I, but God. God will set Pharaoh's mind at ease" (Genesis 41:16 The Message).

We don't see dream interpretation being discussed in the New Testament. But there are many cases of dreams being understood. This indicates that they already had an understanding of how God speaks through dreams. In our case today, we have let go of this and we need to have biblically based instruction to jump-start us into hearing God again through dreams.

Biblical Model Versus Popular Methods

Psychological and many New Age-based models for interpreting dreams will not correctly interpret a dream from God. Many of today's popular methods rely on dream symbols books as opposed to understanding God's symbolic language for you. Jesus said that we must understand parables—and dreams are like night parables.

The popular methods today believe the dream is coming from inside of you, trying to tell you more about yourself. This is not always correct. A biblical understanding of how God speaks to us is that God speaks through His Spirit from the outside in; *from* God *to* you. Popular methods tend to see all dream symbols representing various aspects of you.

To understand a dream, we must allow the Holy Spirit to guide us to the interpretation and application of the dream. There are some symbols and common dreams that tend to be universal in their meaning, but we must always rely on God to speak to us. We use a combination of training to recognize important symbols and allow the Holy Spirit to tell us how they apply.

There are many Christians who believe that God just gives us the meaning and we cannot use interpretation. If you notice, Jesus trained His disciples to understand a parable through continual interpretation and practice. He did not say, "Just let the Holy Spirit tell you." Don't get me wrong, we need the Holy Spirit, but my point is that it is okay to study it.

Four Easy Steps to Dream Interpretation

These are questions to ask yourself as you learn, as opposed to steps:

1. Who or what is the dream about, and to what area of your life does it refer?

2. Is the dream positive or negative; and notice the color scheme: is it bright or dark?

3. Are there any repeated themes, or is it a common dream?

4. What are three or four main points of the dream?

Let's look at these four questions in detail so we can learn how to interpret dreams.

Question 1: Who or what is the dream about?

The very first thing you want to look for when it comes to dreams is who or what the dream is about. Are you the main character, or are you just involved, participating, or observing?

If you are the main character of the dream, the dream is most likely about you. If you are involved or participating, the dream is about you *and* something or someone else. If you are observing a situation in a dream, then most likely the dream is not about you, but about something else completely. Unless of course you are observing yourself, then the dream is still about you.

Observing dreams are usually about someone or something else. People who are particularly compassionate and like to care for others often have observing dreams. This is because they are getting insight on how to pray for people and support them. People with the gift of intercession often have dreams of observing so that they are motivated to pray.

What area of your life is the dream about?

Take note of the area of your life the dream is about. Often there will be people or places in the dream from your family, work, church, etc. Frequently, this will be a clue for context. If you are by yourself or in a place that you do not recognize, then the dream is most likely about you or some aspect of your life.

In addition to the role you play in the dream, it's important to look for the context of your life. Are you by yourself or with your family? Then it's probably mostly about you and having something to do with your family. Are you with people from work or school? Then it probably is related to your career or that area of your life. Are you with people from church or an organization to which you belong? Then the dream most likely relates to that area of your life.

Of course, this is a generalization and does not always apply to every single dream, but it is a good place to start. With all my experience, I have found that most dreams have people or places in them to tell you what area of your life that they point to. I call this a context anchor or clue, and it is helpful to pay attention to these details.

Question 2: Is the dream positive or negative; is the color bright or dark?

The next thing to watch for is if the dream is positive or negative, and whether the colors are bright or dark. This will tell you about the source of the dream. The color of the dream can tell you how to make a practical application to your life. Positive dreams or dreams from God are usually bright or have some colors in them.

The thing that really matters is how you respond. Negative dreams are not all bad as they can reveal things in our lives that need to be changed. Later, you'll learn that when we see a negative dream, we need to flip it around and find the positive side that God is trying to point out. So in a sense, a negative dream can have a positive outcome.

Darker or muted-color dreams tend not to be reality but they can show you things that need to be changed in your life. Black-and-white dreams are usually full of fear and are similar to nightmares. What you should watch for are the dull or muted color dreams, as they are often plans of darkness against your life or maybe your own fears and not reality at all. They are dreams that show you how to pray and how to prepare and plan. Muted-color or dark dreams may not be reality but more of a warning. In many cases, you will need to flip the meaning from negative to recognize a positive outcome.

Do not assume that all color dreams are from God and all black-and-white dreams are negative or from the enemy. There is a lot more to it than that. But we do need to pay attention to whether the dream is positive or negative. That will help us later when we interpret and make a practical application to our daily lives.

People often ask me what a dream symbol means. For instance, they will ask, "What does the color blue mean?" You may want to ask yourself, "Is it blue like the sky of a beautiful sunny day, or is it blue in the eye of a dinosaur that's about to eat me?" There is a big difference and this is called *context*. We will learn more about understanding context and how it can change from dream to dream.

Question 3: Are there repeated themes, or is it a common dream?

Another major thing to watch for is repeated themes. This is the same thing said two times or more. Is the same thing said twice, is the same thing said twice? Did you catch that? I'm repeating myself for dramatic effect. Sometimes themes repeat in a dream in order to highlight something important to pay attention to.

An example would be having a deflated beach ball and then walking to your car and seeing a flat tire. The repeated theme is loss of air. In dreams, air can represent aspects of your spiritual life. This dream may indicate that you need to increase your spiritual connection.

Repeated themes can also occur in different dreams over a period of time. It becomes easier to recognize this once you get into the habit of recording your dreams in a dream journal or on a computer on a regular basis. I will go into more detail on how to record your dreams and tips on journaling later.

Is this a common dream? Watch for dreams like these: flying, falling, running, having a baby, teeth coming loose, etc. The meaning may vary from dream to dream, but it will help you to recognize familiar themes. Many of these common dreams actually have a common meaning. We will study more about common dreams in this chapter and become familiar with the dreams that many people have on a regular basis.

Question 4: What are three or four main points?

If you had to break down the dream to only three or four points, what would they be? These are the main elements of the dream. Though a dream may be quite detailed, find just three or four main points that stand out. Even though there are often more than three or four points to the dream, these main points will help you quickly get the main meaning of the dream. It's like getting the interpretation into the crosshairs of a gun.

Did you know that your brain processes things in summary? If I asked you what you did last weekend, you would probably give me three to four main points and not go into all the details. We tend to summarize when we talk about things that we have done in the past. When Jesus taught parables, He gave simple explanations. Dreams are similar to night parables—we would lose too much of the meaning by looking too closely at the details.

The problem with most new dream interpreters is they get too detailed and try to milk the dream for all it's worth. With dream interpretation, "less is more," especially when you are learning. If you look at all the details in the dream, you will quickly get confused. To be a really good dream interpreter, you need to learn how to distinguish the three or four main points. Then, after you determine the actual interpretation or meaning of the dream, you can get into all the details and what is called the application or the purpose of the dream.

Let's try out this process on a dream.

Flying a Kite Dream

I dreamt that I was with a group of people from school and we were flying kites. A huge wind came and took my kite higher than all the others. I was trying to control the kite when it got tangled in some trees nearby. I was able to fly to the top of the trees and get the kite untangled. Back on the ground again, we all decided to go to the library to study. When we got there, a grand party was going on. I saw a girl I knew from elementary school. She came up and handed me a book and told me I would need this. I woke up.

Let's ask the four questions:

1. Who or what is the dream about, and what area of your life does it refer to?

The dream is about the dreamer and particularly his life involving school.

2. Is the dream positive or negative; and noticing the color, is it bright or dark?

It is a positive dream because even though the kite got stuck in the trees, he was able to get it untangled and the rest of the dream was good.

3. Are there any repeated themes, or is it a common dream?

Yes, there is a repeated theme of flying. He is flying a kite and the dreamer himself flies as well. One of the common dream themes is flying (without an airplane), which indicates a high calling or high creativity.

4. What are the three or four main points of the dream?

The main points of the dream are: flying the kite, the party at the library, and being given a book by the girl.

Common Dreams

The following are a few elements and themes that I have found over the years to be common. Again, the key to interpreting dreams is the Holy Spirit, prayer, and practice. But these can help you get started.

Flying

By far, flying dreams are the most common. Dreams that involve flying without the use of an airplane are usually very positive, depending on context. They indicate you have a high degree of creativity, you have the ability to rise above circumstances and you are possibly maturing spiritually.

Teeth

The second most common dream involves your teeth coming loose or falling out. This type of dream reveals that you are in need of direction. Teeth chew food and make the food useful for the body. Symbolically, teeth chew God's teaching, so it can be digested and made useful through application. Chewing, or thinking about something, brings deeper understanding. That is why teeth coming loose or falling out means that you are in need of direction, wisdom, or advice.

Baby or Pregnant

Both men and women can have this type of dream. Most of the time, it is not a literal dream, but a symbolic one. It is referring to birthing something new into your life. It could be a new job, a gift, an anointing, creativity, or even a clever invention.

Being Naked

Dreaming of having no clothes on in public is a common dream and it is actually positive. It shows that you are open and transparent with others. This could be an indicator of the type of vocation or gifting you have. Most likely, people feel safe around you and they may even talk to you about their problems, meaning you have the ability to help people through counsel or advice.

Being in School

These dreams indicate that you are in a time of learning new things. This is a valuable time of development for your life purpose.

Running or Being Chased

More often than not, dreams that involve running are frightening. This type of dream usually represents one of two situations: you are either running from something in your life, or you are being chased down by your own destiny and it is trying to catch up with you. Either situation can seem scary, because they both require major changes. This type of dream is a strong indication that there is some calling on your life that you have yet to fulfill.

Falling

Dreams in which you are falling indicate that you are out of control in your life. Falling can also suggest that you may need to let go and take some risks. Most people who have falling dreams also have flying dreams. If you are having a repeated falling dream, this indicates you need peace in your life. Once the peace manifests, you can get the creative juices flowing and fly again.

Showing Up Late

Showing up late for anything in a dream is a warning to not miss what is coming. It is just making you aware of something approaching. When you wake up, ask God to help you catch whatever it is.

Not able to Run, Move, or Speak

Whenever you are unable to run or move in a dream, it indicates that something is trying to stop you or hold you back in life. This interpretation can also be applied to dreams when you are not able to speak or cry out for help. This can indicate there are dark forces working against you. But the good news is that there must be something great for you to fulfill, and that is why you are getting so much resistance.

Nightmares or Negative Dreams

Nightmares are similar to the running or being chased dreams. Negative and fearful things are never God's will for your life. Because these types of dreams show the enemy's plans and not God's will, you need to flip them around and begin to pray for the opposite to happen. The only true reality for you is God's intention.

Recurring Dreams

A recurring dream can be an indicator that God wants to either do something new in your life or that He is drawing your attention to change something. Once you either establish the new behavior or take care of the issues, these recurring dreams will stop.

Dreams can provide insight into many areas of your life, such as your destiny and calling or your current self-condition. Even negative dreams and nightmares can turn out positive and encouraging when you learn how to flip a negative dream to get Spirit-inspired strategies.

Understanding hidden messages in dreams and visions will help you take your relationship with God to a new level!

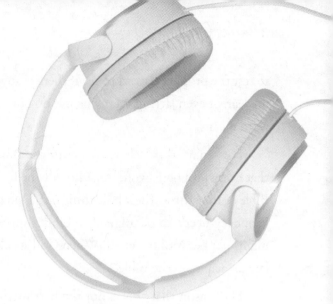

CHAPTER 6

Responding to God's Voice

It helps to realize that simply because God has spoken, it is not somehow *automatic* or guaranteed to happen. When God speaks, it is very important that you understand the timing. In other words, is this for now, or for five years from now?

Also keep in mind that you may need to take into account that the word is coming through your filter or someone else's. Some prophetic words represent God's intention for you, but you will need to contend or battle through to get it.

In First Corinthians 13:9 the apostle Paul says, *"For we know in part and we prophesy in part."* So do not expect the prophetic word to contain everything God wants to say to you. It is also very important that you take the time to *test* the word (1 Thessalonians 5:19–21). It is good to test the prophetic word to see if there is anything in it that is cloudy, unclear, or even jarring. Many people do not understand what testing a word means.

They may ask, "Where is that in the Bible?" because they believe that every prophetic word must literally be found word for word in the Bible or they throw the whole thing out. Don't misunderstand me here. Prophecy needs to be aligned to biblical principles, but sometimes it might not be word for word. When God speaks to us, it will never violate principles in the Bible.

The reason that this is not the best method for testing prophetic words is because it is just too narrow. This way does not take into account all the other ways God uses to speak to us. What we are talking about is discovering a biblical principle for growing in our understanding and not limiting how we will receive that word from God.

Keep in mind, though, that some prophetic words might challenge or stretch us in our understanding. What is most important to remember is that God really does speak and our part is to train ourselves to notice, pray, and then grab hold of it. Prophetic words often require action on our part to activate them.

When God Goes Silent

What if it seems that God has stopped speaking? When we stop hearing God as clearly as we used to, it could be for a few reasons:

- **Negative spin:** focusing on the enemy instead of the Lord.

- **Busyness:** hearing God requires us to slow down and instill peace in our lives.

- **Grumbling or judging others:** I will show you how this closes the heavens over you, and how to open them back up.

- **Previous failure to respond:** God is waiting for us to do the last thing He told us to do, so we stop getting new things.

We need to be very sensitive to how God speaks. If we are not open to all the ways God is speaking to us, we will fail to respond to Him and will soon become dulled to His voice. The more focus we put on hearing God, the more we will see and hear Him. This is like when you buy a certain blue car, and suddenly that is all you see around you.

How People Normally Respond to Hearing God

The following are four normal responses when hearing God:

1. **No response at all:** If you do this consistently, you will eventually close off hearing from God completely.

2. **Over-Assumption:** You assume you know what God is saying, and do not ask how He wants you to respond.

3. **Over-Interpretation:** You take a small amount of revelation that might not be totally clear, and assume you know what it means and make it bigger than it was intended. For example, you have a dream that your best friend had an affair. You confront your friend without realizing the dream was likely symbolic and not literal.

4. **Over-Response:** You make big, important decisions based on a small amount of revelation and little additional confirmation. For example, God speaks to

you that you will have a business that will impact the world. So, in faith, you immediately buy an expensive website domain name before you even have a product. It is much better to start by praying and getting God's timing. You can do something out of faith, but make sure it does not shipwreck you emotionally or financially.

Three Levels of Hearing and Responding

God tends to speak to us on various levels:

- quietly, with subtle impressions or senses;

- more directly, through dreams, visions, or clearly confirming signs; and

- through literal supernatural experiences.

Each level and type of revelation requires a corresponding response. The goal is not necessarily to have higher-level experiences. More importantly, I want you to recognize the weight you can put on what God is saying to you based on the *way* it came to you.

But as a preface, keep this verse in mind as we talk about spiritual experiences:

> *I keep asking that the God of our Lord Jesus Christ, the glorious Father, may give you the Spirit of wisdom and revelation, so that you may know him better* (Ephesians 1:17).

The goal is always to know Him better!

Level 1: Subtle Impressions

You might see a word or a picture in your mind. There may be a subtle sense or leading from God (although this can also indicate a confirmation of a higher-level revelation). You might feel prompted to look up a Bible verse, a song lyric, a work of art, or other media. These are often clues that God uses to lead us into more conversation with Him. You may have a dream that you do not fully understand, or someone might give you a general prophetic word.

These are all examples of lower-level revelations or impressions. They are more symbolic and need more interpretation to understand than higher-level revelations.

Level 2: Clear Leadings

Dreams that "stick with you" after you wake up and the meaning becomes clear very quickly are examples of Level 2 communication from God. For most people, these happen less often than Level 1 types of dreams.

Visions are like watching a movie given only to you. They can be inward, like viewing on a screen inside your head—much like daydreaming. Outward visions appear right before your eyes and give the sense that they are more real than anything else around. Whether experienced as inward or outward, visions tend to be more literal or direct than most dreams.

Angels may come to us in dreams or visions, and often appear as faceless people. Bible verses may come to mind that give clarity to a question or situation and perhaps even confirm an earlier impression. Or you might receive a clear prophetic word from a known prophetic person or a known prophet.

All of these examples have a greater clarity to them and require less interpretation to understand what they mean. But greater humility and wisdom are needed to recognize how to respond when God speaks more clearly!

Level 3: Supernatural Experiences

The Bible is full of stories that describe God's servants having high-level supernatural experiences. Most of them were called to greater levels of influence on earth, so they needed greater levels of revelation to accomplish their God-given life purposes.

For example, Peter was responsible for overseeing the Church in Jerusalem, which was made up of Jewish believers who held to many ancient beliefs and traditions. One day, Peter went into a trance so that God could show him how to see and think differently about people who did not follow Jewish traditions (Acts 10:10). Another time, Peter was busted out of jail by an angel. At first, he thought he was experiencing a vision; then he realized he was literally outside of the jail (Acts 12:6–11).

John wrote that he and others heard God speaking audibly to Jesus (John 12:29). Paul described a time when he was taken into Heaven (2 Corinthians 12:2–4). Philip, one of Jesus' disciples, was physically transported ("translated") from one place to another in an instant (Acts 8:39–40).

Jesus' adoptive father, Joseph, was visited in his dreams multiple times by the angel Gabriel to receive encouragement and guidance from God (Matthew 1:20-21; 2:13-15). A more familiar angelic visitation was Gabriel's visit to Mary, announcing that she was chosen to bear God's own Son (Luke 1:26-38).

All these stories represent God's divine interactions with people He chose to do extraordinary things on earth. The weight of responsibility and degree of influence they carried made it necessary for them to be *very clear* about what God was calling them to say and do for Him and with Him.

There is no need for God to be dramatic when He speaks to us for smaller, daily situations. For instance, my *Daily Prophetic Words* come to me as Level 1 divine impressions from God, and they are often confirmed by Bible verses. I often hear God and get prophetic words through physical signs and living parables in which God speaks using your situation. Repeating a previous example: you get a flat tire and then something else also goes flat. God uses these situations to speak to you about your need for more of His Spirit (represented by air).

Trust God to Guide You through Decisions

> *I will instruct you and teach you in the way you should go;*
> *I will counsel you with my loving eye on you* (Psalm 32:8).

God really is the best Counselor of all. Outside advice from people who have wisdom can help, but be careful to not lean too heavily on the advice of others. You have to weigh it out and get confirmation from God. I urge you to never make a major decision based on one or two pieces of revelation or a vague feeling from God.

In 2001, Linda and I moved to New Hampshire so I could work with prophet John Paul Jackson. I received many prophetic words, dreams, and confirmations. One was a dream that I got a "new hamster," which rhymes with New Hampshire. I knew it was a confirmation, but we did not sell our businesses and move 3,000 miles based on a hamster dream alone.

It still takes faith, and we each must develop a greater level of trust in God as we grow to know Him better.

The "Open Door" Strategy

A mistake people make in trying to hear God for guidance is using the "open door" strategy. Many people pray that God will close all other doors of opportunity except the one they should go through. This may work sometimes, but unfortunately, it does not always happen that way with God. He wants us to become mature in our decision-making.

He will often give us choices in order to train us, the same way an earthly father helps his children. You cannot make decisions for them all their lives, or they will never grow up. A better way to pray is that God would give you the wisdom to know which opportunity or door to take.

The "Fleece Technique"

Another popular method of decision-making is the Judges 6 "fleece technique." Gideon asked God for a sign that He was with him. Gideon laid a fleece of wool on the ground and asked that the fleece would be wet and the ground dry. Sure enough, the next morning he found it wet and the ground dry. So he knew God had answered him.

It is possible for God to answer these types of prayers. "God, if it is Your desire for me to do this, then make this happen … ." But again, God wants us to become mature in our decision-making. Eventually God may not answer this type of prayer, and you will need to rely on other means of determining His will. Unlike Gideon's day, the Holy Spirit is now inside us, and we can know God's will by the amount of peace we have. His peace is the best fleece!

If you are going to use a fleece, be sure to keep a few things in mind: fleeces are a lower, less personal form of revelation, and you will need more confirmation. If you ask God for fleeces often, it indicates that you are operating at a less mature level spiritually. If God has spoken to you clearly, you will not need a fleece to guide you. On something big, understand that He will speak to you through a variety of ways.

How Apostle Paul Heard God

I love to study how people hear God. When I meet someone, I ask them questions and observe their spiritual gifts. Most of the time they are not aware how their gifts operate. But in reality, God speaks to us in many ways and we need to learn how to respond. By studying spiritual gifts and how God speaks, we can master the ability to hear Him more clearly.

I studied how the apostle Paul heard God to shift from being a missionary to going to Rome and fulfilling his destiny by witnessing to Caesar. Initially he said that he felt compelled by the Spirit to go to Jerusalem, not knowing the details. Paul had a direction and strong impression—a Level 1 communication from God.

> *And now, compelled by the Spirit, I am going to Jerusalem, not knowing what will happen to me there. I only know that in every city the Holy Spirit warns me that prison and hardships are facing me* (Acts 20:22–23).

Paul acted on what he felt God directing him to do. On his journey, a prophet named Agabus gave Paul a prophetic word that confirmed his feeling. This was a Level 2 communication.

> *After we had been there a number of days, a prophet named Agabus came down from Judea. Coming over to us, he took Paul's belt, tied his own hands and feet with it and said, "The Holy Spirit says, 'In this way the Jews of Jerusalem will bind the owner of this belt and will hand him over to the Gentiles'"* (Acts 21:10–11).

Paul was later bound by the Romans and handed over to the Jews (Acts 21:30-Acts 22). By today's church standards, some people would call Agabus a false prophet.

When you understand how God speaks, details like this are not always important. We do not want to get legalistic about hearing God and try to do everything with pinpoint accuracy. Remember, we see in part and prophesy in part. All that matters is that we fulfill what God is calling us to do. Too many details can sidetrack us.

> *When we heard this, we and the people there pleaded with Paul not to go up to Jerusalem. Then Paul answered, "Why are you weeping and breaking my heart? I am ready not only to be bound, but also to die in Jerusalem for the name of the Lord Jesus." When he would not be dissuaded, we gave up and said, "The Lord's will be done"* (Acts 21:12–14).

The other believers then realized that Paul was serious about fulfilling what God called him to do and agreed it was God's will. The next night the Lord Himself came and told Paul to go to Rome—a Level 3 supernatural encounter.

> *The following night the Lord stood near Paul and said, "Take courage! As you have testified about me in Jerusalem, so you must also testify in Rome"* (Acts 23:11).

Notice the steps Paul took to fulfill his destiny: He started out feeling compelled. Then he had a sense from God to go to Jerusalem, but did not know the details. As he took steps to fulfill what he was sensing, a well-known prophet (Agabus) confirmed it. This caused Paul to be willing to die if necessary. Finally, the Lord came and told Paul to take courage and go to Rome.

The clearer God speaks, the more difficult time we may have to get into what He is telling us. When Paul (Saul) was on the road to Damascus (Acts 9), God spoke clearly, and Paul went through a rough time to finally become an apostle. Jesus told Peter he would deny Him three times; then Peter went through a difficult time of feeling that he had failed.

This is why God speaks to you most often through unclear dreams and impressions. You will have less warfare and resistance when the message is more veiled. Remember that you do not need the higher-level words and visitations from God for most things He is calling you to do.

CHAPTER 7

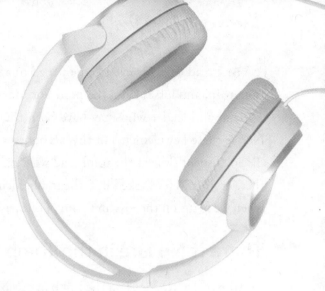

Hearing God Brings Healing

One day I had a breakthrough experience that changed my life forever. I was reading the Bible and noticed that Mary Magdalene went to Jesus' tomb on Sunday morning, *after* He was crucified and buried. The stone in front of the tomb was rolled aside, so she knelt down and looked within, but His body was not there. Mary did not realize that He had been resurrected from the dead. She did not know where He was, and began to cry because of her great loss.

Inside the tomb were two angels who asked her why she was crying. Then behind her came the voice of a man she thought was a gardener—but it was Jesus. When He spoke her name, *"Mary,"* she recognized Him and was ecstatic (John 20:1–16).

As I read this, my eyes were opened to a key for getting over rejection, pain, and losses from the past. For Mary, her pain was the loss of a friend and leader who may have been the first to ever care for her. Notice these key elements of this account in John 20:1–16: The other disciples spent time at the tomb and went back home, but Mary stayed there crying. Mary looked into the tomb, focused on her loss, similar to when we focus on the loss and pain of our past.

There Is No Life in the Tomb

Too often, we focus on the tomb of our past. Yes, there is an appropriate amount of time to deal with grief and loss. But there is also a time to look in a new direction. You cannot live your life at the tomb of your past. Did you notice where Jesus was? He was behind her. Mary had to stand up and turn 180 degrees from the tomb. This symbolizes the need for us to turn our focus away from our past pain and loss.

Notice that Jesus appeared as a gardener. This symbolizes that when you focus on the future, God is there to help things grow and bring life. Also, Mary saw two angels inside the tomb. The symbolism here is that inside every painful experience is a blessing from God, if we can only recognize it.

When Jesus said, *"Mary,"* her eyes were opened and she immediately recognized Him. Oftentimes, we are not able to recognize the work of God in our painful situation. I started to realize that inside every painful experience is a gift. By simply changing your focus, you can allow the past to strengthen you and give you the necessary tools to help others who are camped out at their tombs.

This is an important part of hearing the voice of God. As you develop a close relationship with Him, God will find ways to let you know He loves and cares for you specifically. The power of turning away from the past and negative things is vital to receiving all that God has for us! I bet you did not expect to read this in a book about hearing God, but it is *really* needed. Please do not skip through this, because it will help you advance the most.

Humility

If God is inviting you higher, the name of the road you will need to take for spiritual promotion is called *Humility*. Most people try humbling themselves and suffer from false humility and lack authority as a result. In 2009, I was in that condition until a prophet, Bob Jones, publicly pointed out to me that I was pulling back from releasing prophetic words because of the warfare.

It was a humbling time for me. But I stepped up in the midst of adversity and operated by faith, even though my life was falling apart around me. What I learned is to not back down when the enemy is intimidating you. God will give you the resources, strength, and anointing to break through. Your ability to hear God is always going to be there. You *must* develop godly character so that God can trust you with more.

> *Humble yourselves, therefore, under God's mighty hand, that he may lift you up in due time* (1 Peter 5:6).

The foundation for a strong spiritual life requires being humble. Jesus demonstrated humility. He washed His disciples' feet, seldom defended Himself, and when He could have called in angels to help Him, He took the humble road.

Some characteristics of genuine humility are:

- freely admitting when you are wrong and being quick to apologize;

- having a habit of honesty;

- and being teachable to grow in your spiritual gifts.

If you are truly being humble, you will not get defensive when someone confronts you. You will not deflect what people say to you; instead, you will take it to heart, take time to think and pray about it, and thank them for their honesty.

> *For all those who exalt themselves will be humbled, and those who humble themselves with be exalted* (Luke 14:11).

There is a balance to being humble. You need to use boundaries and recognize certain people who might be unhealthy for you. You do not need to be a doormat or no longer have an opinion, and you do not need to beat yourself up. Do not necessarily believe everything that people say—good or bad.

A spiritual mentor told me, "As God begins to move in your life and give you favor, don't believe all the good things that people say about you." I'll add, "Yes, receive it! But do not let it go to your head." One of the ways I stay humble is to tell people my weaknesses—something few leaders do. But it works for me to stay humble. I do not want people to think that all my problems are over, and that I do not struggle. We will always be struggling with something!

False humility is when you do not use your spiritual gifts or help people because you are trying to stay humble. This is the biggest attack against Christians today. They are constantly being told to stay humble, so they do not step out at all. This is false humility.

Pride

> *Do not think of yourself more highly than you ought, but rather think of yourself with sober judgment, in accordance with the faith God has distributed to each of you* (Romans 12:3).

Pride is the opposite of humility. It is seeing yourself greater than you actually are. The tricky thing about pride is that it blinds you to reality. When you have pride, you are usually the last one to know it. The deadly combination of pride and lack of humility will delay you from reaching your destiny. If not dealt with, it could cause you to miss your destiny completely because you are open to deception.

Symptoms of pride include being self-centered and demanding, self-promoting, unteachable and uncorrectable, judgmental or critical of others, overly sarcastic, and quick to cut others down (even with humor). When you have pride, you tend to make excuses for your behavior. If you are not able to be corrected appropriately or receive instruction, you will never grow and learn.

The best way to remove pride is to recognize it when it is happening or has happened. Confess it as sin, ask forgiveness from God, and move on. Listen to me: God will allow all of us to experience pride at one time or another in our lives so that we will recognize it. In my book *Spiritual Identity Theft Exposed,* I talk about how the enemy works with both pride and humility. If we get prideful, we can over-respond and become falsely humble by "dying" too hard! Quite often, God will give us a passion or strong desire to fulfill something in our lives. But many people do not reach their destiny because they have over-responded to pride and "died to" or abandoned any desire they may have once had. God wants to give us good things. Once our motives are right, He can do this without limit.

> *Take delight in the Lord, and he will give you the desires of your heart* (Psalm 37:4).

Christians often quote the Bible verse, *"He must become greater; I must become less"* (John 3:30). The problem with false humility is when you try to become less without allowing God's character and gifts in you to become greater, you end up empty. "Dying to yourself" means that the motives and intentions of your heart are no longer self-focused, but have become God-focused.

Rejection

The fear of being rejected causes you to recoil and withdraw. It is crippling. Sadly, like most of these issues, you are usually not aware that you are suffering from it. Fear of rejection will hinder you from making decisions and taking risks, and will stop you from being all that you were created to be.

Rejection usually starts at a young age. We begin to feel powerless to change a situation or afraid of confrontation. As a coping mechanism, we run and hide when we are hurt. But later in life, running and hiding no longer serve us, and we need to get rid of that mindset. The scary part is that many people suffering from rejection think they are being humble by not speaking out, which is false humility.

Symptoms of rejection include: isolating yourself; getting angry at people who do not agree with you; shutting down and not speaking your opinion, even though it bothers you. You may have a history of changing jobs or churches because you get offended. You may also avoid taking direction from those in authority.

Healing from rejection comes with searching your own heart and asking God to reveal any of these tendencies. To get through rejection, we must practice forgiveness and humility.

Healing Strategy

I first discovered how to receive a healing strategy when I had to leave pastoring in 2001. I had Huntington's disease, which is fatal and had killed many of my family members. I got radically healed after God showed me a strategy for how to go after it like it was my full-time job.

I noticed that Jesus seldom healed the same way twice. As I studied this, I recognized that Jesus knew God's strategy for each person's healing. (See Luke 4:40, John 9:6, Matthew 8:8, and Mark 9:29, to name a few.) One time He laid hands on someone, another time He spit on the ground and made mud to put on the person's eyes. The next time He just said the word, and another time He mentioned that some need prayer and fasting to receive their healing.

I also asked God for a strategy to be healed from Lyme disease when I contracted it a few years ago. It began by having a group of people praying with me seven days a week—sometimes more than once a day—for five months. We would ask God to show us what the enemy did not want us to see. We got specific strategies and followed up with them, such as spiritually cutting off generational connections to sickness.

We saw that there was demonic oppression, or spiritual warfare, coming against me because of what I was trying to accomplish for the Kingdom. We prayed for strategies to deal with my physical health, and asked God for a holistic approach that included my body, soul, and spirit. Some sicknesses have so many different origins and connections that they need to be dealt with in layers or steps.

If you need to be healed, ask God for a strategy, make a list, and begin to go through it. God can heal you *today* from diabetes, but if you do not stop eating sugar and have other unhealthy habits, there is a good chance that you will get sick again. We need to work hand-in-hand with God through the Holy Spirit, and not give up.

After being sick with Lyme disease for over two years, I realized that when we are sick, it is sometimes hard to get up the energy to pursue our own healing at the level needed. That is where our friends and family can come in and help us. Get prayer everywhere you go. Get a strategy from God. Get a breakthrough in your healing.

I was healed of Lyme disease in February 2014. A short time later, I was sick again with an acute case of Multiple Chemical Sensitivity. For three years I went on battling various afflictions, but I got a breakthrough encounter and the Lord gave me the strategy to get set free. I am happy to report that I am now totally healed, though it did not come all at once.

If you are not seeing results in any area of your life, you need to press in until you do. People line up to argue with me, saying that we just need to "claim we are healed" in Jesus' name. Listen to me: I have been healed of a lot of things using prayer and the word of faith with the name of Jesus. But when it was not working, I pressed in and asked for a healing strategy. Sometimes we can have a full healing all at once and other times we have to walk it out.

My mom and my aunt were two amazing women of faith. They both received prayer for Huntington's disease and stood strong in faith that they were healed—but there was no evidence of it in their lives. They both died before their time in 1999. I do not know about you, but I am sick and tired of being sick and tired, and of financial losses, debt, and setbacks!

My Healing Strategy

There is no formula to get healed, and I am not trying to create a method. All I know is that the following strategy has worked for three major diseases in my life:

- Take communion and anoint yourself with oil daily. Begin praying daily for yourself and your situation. Ask God to show you what the devil does not want you to see about the situation. Take notes and respond to what you are hearing. Find a team, even just a couple of people, to pray with you—daily if possible.

- Stop doing things that harm your body. Use wisdom and ask God to show you what to do physically. At one point with Lyme disease, we anointed my medications with oil and broke off the side effects. I also changed my diet and supplements based on prophetic dreams. I recommend using natural healing when possible. For me, essential oils are a big part of my healing strategy.

Go to as many healing meetings as you can. You can pray over your finances at a healing service as well. Do *not* leave church without getting prayer. Contact ministries in your area or online that specialize in healing prayer. Go to the healing rooms and get prayer *every* time they offer it. Some healing rooms even offer prayer through Skype or over the phone.

If you want to know and understand the full update to how I have been healed, I have an online workshop called *Accelerating Your "Time to Heal."* I go into all the details of how I got set free and developed a healing strategy for each of the most prevalent afflictions people are suffering from today. I pulled together my experience and several years of study and research on the subject. You can find this on my website.

Dr. Henry Wright's book, *A More Excellent Way,* has a very helpful section about the "spiritual roots" to disease. I do not necessarily agree with everything in his book, but he does a great job of describing how to identify and remove spiritual connections that have caused hereditary illnesses in you and your family. You may need to repeat his process more than once, because God often reveals these issues in "layers" to keep us from becoming overwhelmed.

Many people with higher callings get judged or cursed by those who do not understand or are jealous. Rick Joyner's booklet *Overcoming Witchcraft,* is a good resource to better understand the spiritual effects of judging, cursing, and jealousy. In addition to physical illness, you might also experience confused thinking, depression, hopelessness, discouragement, or other negative feelings. Ask God to show you what is causing your symptoms and how to remove the effects from your mind and body.

This might sound strange, but it worked for me several times. If you cannot hear God for your breakthrough, try driving thirty-five to fifty miles away from your home to pray. Demons often have authority over a thirty-five to fifty-mile radius. If you feel different and can hear clearly after leaving your area, you will need to break the demonic assignment against you in your community.

Create declaration prayers for wholeness: *"You will also declare a thing, it will be established for you; so light will shine on your ways"* (Job 22:28 NKJV). Find some Bible verses and lines from prophetic words God has spoken over you. My staff and I wrote the following declarations for my healing, which we based on Bible verses and prophetic words over my life:

> *I declare and decree full healing from all the effects of this attack on my body, soul, and spirit.*
>
> *I speak peace over any trauma and anxiety that may have come in from past wounds and abuses, and bring total and complete healing.*
>
> *I declare a clear mind and emotions as I enter into God's rest.*
>
> *I call in all the heavenly provision needed to live a healthy and spiritually rich life.*

I ask you, God, to reveal Your love and intentions. Reveal Your perfect will for me and my complete healing. I thank You even now for this process and its completion.

I declare that no weapon formed against me shall prosper! Thank you, God, that You are more than able to do all that we ask, think, or imagine.

In the power of Jesus' name, amen.

CHAPTER 8

Lifestyle of Hearing God

Prophetic Life Parables

Let's transition into an aspect of hearing God that not many people teach on. Sometimes God uses everyday events in your life, like a living parable, to speak a message to you or for someone else.

For a number of years I did not realize I had this gift. In fact, I sometimes thought I was crazy when, out of the blue, I would have unusual thoughts come into my head, or things would happen to me that were way out of my normal experience. The light went on for me when I was speaking at an event with a friend. We were sharing a hotel room, and he told me he had forgotten to pack his pajamas. He never forgets his pajamas!

We discussed the prophetic and symbolic significance of forgetting pajamas, and determined that God must be speaking a message to this church—they were lacking intimacy with Him. Sure enough, we ministered along those lines and saw a great breakthrough that weekend. I started to notice that this was going on in my life as well. This is very biblical, because the prophets of the Old Testament often lived out prophetic words for Israel.

Examples of Living Parables

I was traveling to Canada on an unexpected ministry trip. My wife found that we had 6 dollars in Canadian coins, and gave them to me before I left. I sat in seat number 6 on both flights to get there, and we arrived at gate 66. My hosts had arranged for me to stay at Motel 6. Most people would think that 666 is not a good thing. But with God, it is best not to assume anything!

I knew this was a prophetic word for the church, so I prayed. I heard the Lord say that six years ago He promised them something and now, in the seventh year, the new thing was going to come, but they needed to labor for it. The number six represents human effort. Sometimes we need to press in and labor for the things of God. Sure enough, this is exactly what was going on.

Another time, I was traveling to a particular city on a short, nonstop flight. The airline lost my bag, which was unusual because I pray so much to not miss flights or lose my bags. So I knew God was speaking. I shopped for some clothes since I had to speak the next day. Two days later, it was Sunday and my bag still had not arrived. I was scheduled to speak that morning, so I walked two miles in the rain to get to the local Walmart. By the time I got back to my hotel, my bag was sitting there waiting for me. I had only twenty minutes to get ready to speak that Sunday morning.

The prophetic word for the church was, "Do not lose something that is dear to you. God is calling you to something new, and you will be tempted to settle for something less. But stick with it because, at the last minute, God will open it up for you and it will be double."

I have story after story of living parables like these that most people miss unless they are pointed out. To recognize if you are living out a prophetic message from God, ask God to speak to you through natural things. Notice when things start going wrong or are out of the ordinary, and look for the symbolic meaning. Begin to notice the news or events in your community. What could the deeper prophetic meaning be?

When you get strange thoughts in your head that do not seem to be yours, you are probably picking up on the spiritual realm in the community, or for someone sitting close to you. Use this as a heads-up to pray.

God Speaks without Audible Words

Many of the Old Testament prophets lived out prophetic words. Jeremiah and Isaiah lived out prophetic messages from God, and Hosea's entire life was a prophetic parable. God instructed them to say and do very radical things to turn Israel back to God. Today He is leading us to do more prophetic acts of kindness than acts of judgment.

Sometimes God speaks symbolically, using natural events that represent supernatural things. The Bible is filled with examples: God put a rainbow in the sky after the great flood; He caused earthquakes and storms at just the right time; He sometimes spoke audibly, but His voice sounded like thunder. Jesus Himself sometimes lived out prophetic parables. For example, consider how He responded in the storms.

There were two storms that came against the disciples' boat, both of which were designed to kill Jesus and His disciples. In Matthew 8, Jesus slept while the disciples thought they were going to die. They woke Him up, He spoke to the storm, and it stopped. In Matthew 14, a storm came against the boat again. This time Jesus walked on the water. Both times, Jesus performed a dramatic prophetic act to demonstrate how to respond during difficult times. Sometimes you need to rise and walk above your circumstances. Other times you need to sleep and rest during the storms. But as He says, do not be afraid.

I have already talked about Agabus, but take another look:

> *Coming over to us, he took Paul's belt, tied his own hands and feet with it and said, "The Holy Spirit says, 'In this way the Jewish leaders in Jerusalem will bind the owner of this belt and will hand him over to the Gentiles'"* (Acts 21:11).

That is another biblical example of a prophetic act or life parable.

The Open Heaven Lifestyle

I am describing a lot of supernatural things because I want to clear the spiritual air over you and create an open heaven to hear God. Remember, our motivation and foundation for hearing God is *"so that you may know him better"* (Ephesians 1:17).

The phrase "open heavens" is used often in the Bible. For example, God opens the heavens over your work and money:

> *The Lord will open the heavens, the storehouse of his bounty, to send rain on your land in season and to bless all the work of your hands. You will lend to many nations but will borrow from none* (Deuteronomy 28:12).

God opened Heaven over Peter and radically changed his theology. His revelation opened the Gentiles, or non-Jewish people, to receive the Gospel of Jesus:

> *About noon the following day as they were on their journey and approaching the city, Peter went up on the roof to pray. He became hungry and wanted something to eat, and while the meal was being prepared, he fell into a trance. He saw heaven opened and something like a large sheet being let down to earth by its four corners. It contained all kinds of four-footed animals, as well as reptiles and birds. Then a voice told him, 'Get up, Peter. Kill and eat'"* (Acts 10:9–13).

God is still doing these things today, but most people are missing it.

There are places on earth that feel more open spiritually than others. Jesus went to the Mount of Olives to pray—this was an open heaven or spiritual place for Jesus. God told Elijah to go to Mount Horeb and He would speak to him (1 Kings 19). Moses went to Mount Sinai. The heavens opened at Jesus' baptism: *"When all the people were being baptized, Jesus was baptized too. And as he was praying, heaven was opened"* (Luke 3:21).

I have personally felt open heavens at a prayer mountain in Seoul, South Korea, in Redding, California, and when I lived in Moravian Falls, North Carolina and Santa Maria, California. I experienced more angelic activity in Santa Maria than any other place I have been on earth. Understand that you do not have to go to these places to hear God, unless He tells you to go. You can have an open heaven over your city, business, church, house, or yourself. Pay attention to where you feel more creative or encouraged. Chances are there is something significant about those places for you.

Some places are closed off and hard to connect with God. This may be because it was once an open heaven, but was closed off by the occult or negative prayers happening there, like Sedona, Arizona. One of the hardest places for me to hear God has been around some of the Ivy League colleges like Harvard, because the collective spirit of intellect gathered there makes it difficult for me. Some people can hear God in these places, though, based on their gifts and calling.

Your Own "Open Heaven"

Have you ever been around people who seem to "carry" a strong and peaceful presence of God? There is a good chance that they have a flow from Heaven over them. Most people think that opening God's Heaven for more revelation and blessing involves repenting of sin and doing things like fasting and praying. I was doing this, and that can be part of it. But the mistake people make is constantly focusing on their sin and trying to become sinless, which puts them in a negative spin. Constantly focusing on what is wrong will close the heavens over you. Yes, repent of sin, but know there is more.

What I have found for myself and the tens of thousands of people I have coached and trained, is that we need to get rid of a few things (in addition to the obvious) so that we can get a clear connection with God. Not loving people, grumbling and complaining, speaking against others instead of praying for them, judging and cursing instead of blessing—these things are contrary to God's Word and are not the fruit of the Spirit.

Somehow these small things slip under the radar and are not considered sins, or at least we do not see them as "big" sins. But these very things will clog your spiritual perception. For the longest time, I felt like things were closed over me. I could hear God due to my spiritual gifts, but it took a lot of effort and things were not flowing consistently for me. I asked God what I needed to do to hear Him more consistently and experience His power and presence regularly. I was shocked when He told me to stop grumbling.

I did not understand how dramatically that word from God would change things in my life. After all, I had been a Christian for a couple of decades. I had been in ministry and witnessed God flow through me and do miracles that I could not deny were God's power. Would complaining actually close the heavens over me? God spoke to me to stop complaining and start blessing. It did not happen right away, but very soon things started to change.

I traveled a lot and was complaining that I often got stuck in the back of the plane in row sixty-six, seat six. God told me to be grateful and watch what would happen. So I started making an effort to be grateful, no matter what happened to me. It was not easy at first, and felt unnatural. But there is something about praise and thankfulness that brings you into agreement with Heaven.

I started to understand the verse *"My grace is sufficient"* in Second Corinthians 12:9. A short time later, I started getting free upgrades to first class, received better customer service, and enjoyed friendlier, more peaceful times in general. It took a few months, but the spiritual atmosphere began to shift over me. I even started hearing God more clearly for other people.

As I studied this more, I realized that there were actually major keys or components to opening the heavens around me and allowing blessing to flow to me—and everyone who believes. The following four keys are what I discovered: love, grace, gratitude, and generosity.

Love, Grace, Gratitude, and Generosity

Jesus said that the most powerful thing we can do is *love* God, our neighbor, and ourselves:

> Jesus replied: "'Love the Lord your God with all your heart and with all your soul and with all your mind.' This is the first and greatest commandment. And the second is like it: 'Love your neighbor as yourself.' All the Law and the Prophets hang on these two commandments" (Matthew 22:37–40).

I had read those verses many times, but suddenly they came alive to me. I had never noticed the three "loves" Jesus spoke about: love God (with all your heart), love your neighbor, and love yourself. Love is so powerful, and I will show you later how it is the key to getting a breakthrough in your life.

It baffles me how we can read Jesus' words and watch as He demonstrated unconditional love, and yet can be guilty of speaking against people who are different from us. We need to love people who have different beliefs, belong to different political parties, and embrace lifestyles that are different from ours. Yes, we need to love all people as ourselves.

The second key is *grace,* which is cutting people slack instead of cutting them down, having patience and being understanding. Next is *gratitude,* which is being thankful for everything instead of complaining, blessing and not cursing, and paying it forward on a regular basis. Last, we have *generosity,* which is not just giving money, but also our time, energy, and resources. I will often pay more for something than it is worth just to bless a person. Tip big and give away without expecting it back. It all boils down to love, thankfulness, and giving freely.

The reason these four keys are so important is because of the spiritual principle of sowing and reaping: *"Do not be deceived: God cannot be mocked. A man reaps what he sows"* (Galatians 6:7). Most people think this is talking about sin—when you do bad things, bad things come to you—but it is way more complex than that. It applies to nearly all areas of your life. The more you sow good things—like love, thankfulness, and giving freely—the more you will reap these things into your life.

Jesus was pretty clear when He said, *"Bless those who curse you, pray for those who mistreat you"* (Luke 6:28). When we get angry and curse back, we end up coming into agreement with darkness. Remember, when we agree together, it will be done (Matthew 18:19). We want to agree with Heaven over a person or situation and not agree with cursing. This is a major principle to grasp if you want to hear God clearly and flow with the Holy Spirit.

Change Your Spiritual Atmosphere

You *can* radically change your life in thirty days or less. Most people get motivated to do something when they are angry or dissatisfied. If you receive bad customer service, your displeasure might motivate you to complain. Try being motivated by good things as well. I am not saying that we can no longer complain, but when we do, we need to find ways to offset that negative experience with something positive.

Remember, Jesus said to *"bless those who mistreat you."* Find ways to compliment people, encourage them and lift them up, and see what happens to you in return. Of course, you have to really mean it and not do it to get something in return. When I file a complaint, I try to find a few other places that I can bless. I use yelp.com or tripadvisor.com to file lots of compliments and only occasional complaints.

Make a decision now to do good and positive things for others and yourself. What you sow, you will reap. The more you give, the more you receive. Most people are reaping a closed heaven, or inability to hear God, because they are not sowing or doing anything to hear His voice.

The very area where you need the breakthrough is the area where you need to sow or give. Most people understand this with money, but

Jesus said if you give while having something against someone, it is better to leave your money at the altar and go reconcile:

> *Therefore, if you are offering your gift at the altar and there remember that your brother or sister has something against you, leave your gift there in front of the altar. First go and be reconciled to them; then come and offer your gift* (Matthew 5:23–24).

The Spirit of blessing and reconciliation will bring the spiritual breakthrough you need. If you are giving money and not seeing a return, then check your relationships and lifestyle of blessing in other areas of your life.

In Luke 19, a tax collector named Zacchaeus, who had extorted people, had a radical encounter with Jesus. Zacchaeus gave back four times the amount he had stolen. It is not required to do this, but it shows that there are times we need to shift the spiritual atmosphere. I tried taking this literally in my life years ago, and went into debt trying to repay. God does not want us to get legalistic about it. But we can begin to live a lifestyle of blessing that will outweigh the negative.

> *Here is a simple, rule-of-thumb guide for behavior: Ask yourself what you want people to do for you, then grab the initiative and do it for them. Add up God's Law and Prophets and this is what you get* (Matthew 7:12 The Message).

Be aware of what you are sowing on a regular basis. Identifying recurring themes in your daily life can reveal symptoms of what you are sowing into your personal atmosphere. Look for repeated situations, like frequent mistakes in your order or getting a lot of traffic tickets. Maybe good things happen more often for you, like getting an unexpected check in the mail right before your car breaks down.

The way you deal with others sets the tone for how things go for you. If you do find yourself having to complain, make an intentional effort to give at least two compliments first. If you tend to look for people's mistakes, start looking for good things you can report to the manager. You could even write a positive comment for them on social media or Yelp. And tip big. Bless people with money, compliments, gift cards, or words of encouragement. Do not leave a Bible tract; or worse yet, a phony $20 bill tract. They make people mad.

One way to remove negativity from your atmosphere is to stop listening to negative things like talk radio, or reading and watching videos that are negative about leaders or the government. Most people are worried about guarding their "eye gate," but we need to guard our "ear gates" as well. I cannot stress this enough. Step away from the negative chatter from others and on the internet!

Most people are waiting for God to open the heavens over them, but there are things that He is waiting for us to do—find ways to give love and encouragement. Give your time and attention to really listen to people. Things like these will indeed open the heavens over you.

I challenge you to fast from negativity for the next three weeks. When you find yourself thinking negative thoughts about something or someone, turn it into a prayer. You do not have to agree with a person to bless them. When you catch yourself speaking anything negative, do not just shut up—step up and bless.

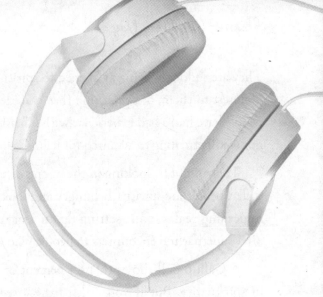

CHAPTER 9

Prophecy and Evangelism

A New Spiritual Hunger

It is easy to notice a new spiritual hunger in people. Television shows talk openly about spiritual things, and psychics are now in plush offices and kiosks at malls. It is not unusual for a high school student to be part of a Wiccan coven, or to browse the occult section of a bookstore looking up spells and incantations. With this increase in occult and spiritual interest, questions must be asked: Why is this happening? Did dark spiritual forces suddenly invade the minds of people?

I believe it is God Himself who has planted this spiritual hunger, and people are now searching for understanding and spiritual fulfillment.

They are suddenly being awakened to spirituality and turning to what is closest to them, or something they can identify with. Because many people have had a bad experience with Christianity or religion, they are not readily turning to a church for help.

They might be looking in the wrong directions, but the good news is that people are spiritually hungry and looking for an encounter with something real. God is setting up an amazing opportunity for us to offer supernatural encounters to people who are hungry for more.

A Gallup poll shows that 84 percent of Americans are interested in spirituality. But if you talk to these seekers, most of them find church and Christianity to be boring and irrelevant. We really need to do something!

I was one of the early forerunners in training and introducing people in the United States to prophetic evangelism. My wife and I planted several churches and trained outreach teams that have had positive results in reaching people with God's love. I specialize in reaching people who are turned off by church, but still want an encounter with God. I made some interesting discoveries.

We Need a Paradigm Shift

God is doing something new. To have empowering encounters will require forgetting some former things we were taught and have been used to doing. Sadly, Christians today do not have the *"eyes to see"* that those older ways are not working to reach people for God. Instead, they are turning people off.

The old paradigm of sharing God's love is actually based on a model that worked more than fifty years ago. People are changing, so we need to change the way we share the message of Jesus. Maybe you have heard people say, "I'm spiritual, but not religious," or "That might be truth for you, but it's not for me." We need to listen to what they are saying, and gear our conversations and encounters based on their current beliefs.

We need to consider how to communicate with people so they can receive from us. Previously, people responded to program-oriented, pre-packaged ways of doing church. Nowadays, we need to be more organic, and our methods need to change based on the people we are interacting with at any given time.

A New Kind of Encounter

People often have a wall up when we try to talk with them about God, but there are things we can do to remove it. Do something positive for them, such as practical acts of kindness. Give them food, money, or something they need. Give them simple, encouraging words, which is prophecy spoken in nonreligious language. It is very powerful to give people prophetic words in a language they can understand. Give them encouraging words of knowledge from God. Interpret their dreams. Pray for their healing.

God's Job Versus Ours

Jesus told His followers, *"As I have loved you, so you must love one another"* (John 13:34), and the Holy Spirit will come and convict people of guilt in regard to sin (John 16:8). God's task is to convict people of sin. Ours is to love people. We get it backward when we try to convict people of sin instead of loving them. We try to do God's job instead of ours, derailing our encounters with people in need of God's love.

These beginning chapter paragraphs you just read contain huge revelations. Take a moment and think about what you read. If guilty of anything, it is time to change our minds (repent) and our actions.

WWJD: What Would Jesus Do?

I thoroughly studied and researched all the encounters in the New Testament that Jesus or His disciples had with those who were *not* believers. I was very surprised at what I found. I am not talking about the encounters He had with the religious crowd, like the Pharisees or teachers of the Law, but with unbelievers in the streets.

I discovered two important points: 1) Jesus was only angry with religious people who followed God but were mean-spirited and did not have God's heart for people, 1, and 2) Jesus did not use the verses we use to share God's love with people.

We need new kinds of encounters with people to open them up instead of close them off. Many of our familiar approaches have left people with a wall raised between their hearts and well-meaning Christians. This is unfortunate because God wants to speak to people today. We have to take into consideration some of their beliefs and values, and gear our conversations and prophetic words along those lines. When we do this, it opens people up to God.

I have found that these new, encouraging types of encounters— using the prophetic gifts, dream interpretation, and interpreting body art—are incredibly effective.

We Need Eyes to See the Culture

I keep talking about having *"eyes to see and ears to hear"* because it is something Jesus spoke on more than any other subject. I was in a coffee shop, and God gave me a prophetic word for the woman behind the counter. I call this an "over the counter encounter." I asked her if she had been having "flying dreams." She said, "No, but I have a dream to fly." She wanted to become a pilot, but she had failed the test because her eyesight was bad. My question got her attention, and we were able to minister to and encourage her!

If we are to have eyes to see and ears to hear, as Jesus said, we must understand the culture and how to speak and prophesy into it. For instance, remember to be sensitive to people. If they are working behind the counter, they might get in trouble if you hold up the line to pray for them. You might have to come back later.

I believe we need to become modern-day missionaries. A missionary will study the language and culture, and learn to communicate the message of Jesus in a way they can understand, starting from what people already believe. Many people today do not believe in one absolute truth. So telling them Jesus is the only way to God and quoting John 14:6 is not necessarily a good icebreaker. Save it for later.

> *Jesus answered, "I am the way and the truth and the life. No one comes to the Father except through me"* (John 14:6).

A more effective approach would be to start with something in common with them, such as an interest to hear from God or understand dreams. To prove my point, if you tell someone that you are a Christian and have a word from God for them, a common response might be, "So do you believe Jesus is the only way to God?" This usually creates a wall, argument, or debate about truth. A more effective way to open them up to God is to show them that God indeed still speaks today.

A Closer Look at John 14:6

For a new slant on John 14:6, notice the order of Jesus' words. He is *the way*, then *the truth*, and then *the life*. I want to credit this amazing revelation to my friend, Rob Mazza. If you show people *the way* by doing something practical, then *the truth* will soon come to them, and they will eventually get into new *life*.

Starting out by showing people the ways of God is much easier—and a lot more fun! It gives you freedom to be real and hang out with them without feeling like you have to "turn every conversation to God." It also allows for a natural, organic process to take place in your relationships.

When we start with the truth in our conversations, we get the cart before the horse. Notice in the book of Acts that the early movement was called *"the Way"* (Acts 9:2). So the earliest believers must have understood this principle.

How God Can Empower You

Let's look at our Source of the power:

> But you will receive power when the Holy Spirit comes on you; and you will be my witnesses in Jerusalem, and in all Judea and Samaria, and to the ends of the earth (Acts 1:8).

We must have God's Holy Spirit and power. Power can be demonstrated through love, practical acts of kindness, healing, prophecy, or just being nice to a person who has been wounded.

Now take a look at when this power came for the first time:

> In the last days, God says, I will pour out my Spirit **on all people**. Your sons and daughters will prophesy, your young men will see visions, your old men will dream dreams. Even on my servants, both men and women, I will pour out my Spirit in those days, and they will prophesy (Acts 2:17–18).

It is interesting that prophecy, dreams, and visions will become more prevalent as time progresses. We are seeing this today! We really need to open people's eyes spiritually.

Opening Their Eyes

In Acts 9, Saul (later renamed Paul) had an encounter with Jesus on the road to Damascus. He was blinded for three days and was radically converted! He went on to write most of the New Testament and started churches worldwide. Later on, as he was recounting this to King Agrippa, he told more of the story. This is Jesus speaking to him during the "road to Damascus" experience:

> *I will rescue you from your own people and from the Gentiles. I am sending you to them to open their eyes and turn them from darkness to light, and from the power of Satan to God, so that they may receive forgiveness of sins and a place among those who are sanctified by faith in me* (Acts 26:17–18).

With all my training over the years, no one had ever told me of the need to open people's eyes to God. Let's take a look at how Jesus interacted with two key people. These are two encounters Jesus had with unbelieving people that totally opened their eyes.

> *When Jesus saw Nathanael approaching, he said of him, "Here truly is an Israelite in whom there is no deceit." "How do you know me?" Nathanael asked. Jesus answered, "I saw you while you were still under the fig tree before Philip called you." Then Nathanael declared, "Rabbi, you are the Son of God; you are the king of Israel"* (John 1:47–49).

Jesus used a word of knowledge to get Nathanael's attention, and it worked. Nathanael said, *"How do you know me?"* indicating it was an accurate word. Jesus used the prophetic to open Nathanael's eyes and, most important, Jesus encouraged him by calling him an honorable man.

Then Jesus had a conversation with a Samaritan woman.

> He told her, "Go, call your husband and come back." "I have no husband," she replied. Jesus said to her, "You are right when you say you have no husband. The fact is, you have had five husbands, and the man you now have is not your husband. What you have just said is quite true." "Sir," the woman said, "I can see that you are a prophet" (John 4:16–19).

When she acknowledged Jesus was a prophet, it was her way of confirming that her spiritual eyes had been opened. (Today, people will say, "Are you a psychic?") This was one radical encounter with Jesus! He used a word of knowledge to get her attention, and then He found something positive in her and called her honest.

Did you catch that? He called an adulterous woman honest. I have had people argue with me that Jesus judged her, but He did not at all. Jesus was very encouraging! He found something positive in the person. We need to do this as well.

Understanding the Process

People tend to encounter God best through a process of circumstances, and it often takes more than one encounter. When we are talking about planting seeds, this includes giving prophetic words, not just sharing God's love with them.

In the Bible, Matthew and Mark both included Jesus' parable about a farmer who went out and planted seeds (Mark 4:3–8; Matthew 13:3-9). As the seeds were scattered, they fell in various places and began to grow based on the conditions surrounding the seeds. In Matthew 13:19–23, Jesus explained that the seeds represent the message about the Kingdom of Heaven. In Mark's account, Jesus went on to describe how the message of the Kingdom of Heaven grows in people's hearts like seeds.

> He also said, "This is what the kingdom of God is like. A man scatters seed on the ground. Night and day, whether he sleeps or gets up, the seed sprouts and grows, though he does not know how. All by itself the soil produces grain— first the stalk, then the head, then the full kernel in the head. As soon as the grain is ripe, he puts the sickle to it, because the harvest has come" (Mark 4:26–29).

Notice the process the seed goes through: *"All by itself the soil produces grain."* The seed sprouts, grows a stalk, a head, then the full kernel, and it ripens until it is ready to be harvested! When we give people prophetic words, we need to recognize this process and not expect a "harvest" on every encounter.

It is better to be low-key and look for divine opportunities to talk about God in a nonreligious and nonconfrontational way. This is why it is so important to develop relationships with people who do not know God. Hang out with them, pray for them, and wait for God to open doors of opportunity.

Speaking Nonreligious

It is very important to be able to speak to people using language they can understand. If we do not, they will put up a barrier, and we will not be able to reach them for God.

The apostle Paul knew it was important to speak to people this way:

> *Pray diligently. Stay alert, with your eyes wide open in gratitude. ... Pray that every time I open my mouth I'll be able to make Christ plain as day to them. Use your heads as you live and work among outsiders. Don't miss a trick. Make the most of every opportunity. Be gracious in your speech. The goal is to bring out the best in others in a conversation, not put them down, not cut them out* (Colossians 4:2–6 The Message).

When we attempt to talk to someone with no religious background using religious words and phrases, we might as well be speaking another language. Paul addressed this issue again to the people in Corinth:

> *Unless you speak intelligible words with your tongue, how will anyone know what you are saying? You will just be speaking into the air. Undoubtedly there are all sorts of languages in the world, yet none of them is without meaning. If then I do not grasp the meaning of what someone is saying, I am a foreigner to the speaker, and he is a foreigner to me* (1 Corinthians 14:9–11).

We have found that people are very open to talking about God, particularly when we use language they can understand. There are two main reasons you will want to learn to communicate without sounding religious:

1. Many people no longer have a religious background and may not know what we are saying. Unlike the past, there are many people with no memory of Christianity in their lives, so they do not have a context for the Bible or our jargon.

2. When we come across people who have had a religious background, we oftentimes find that they have

been wounded by a legalistic, non-loving approach to Christianity. So when we talk with them, they close off instead of open up. We want to be the salt of the earth, but as we share about God using religious language, we can instead be salt in people's wounds.

People today are beaten down, stressed out, worried, afraid, tired, and fed up. They need encouragement. Be sure to speak in nonreligious language because people do not always know what we are talking about. Instead of asking them if they want a prophetic word, we can change our approach and call them encouraging words or spiritual readings.

Prophecy for Believers Versus Unbelievers

Here are some tips for giving prophetic words to people who are Christians as opposed to those who are not. This is learning to prophesy to people inside the church versus others.

Believers	Others
Speak openly and use the Bible as a reference.	Be careful how you speak so they will understand and receive you. They may close off when you mention the Bible, so tell them the principles without quoting the verse and reference.
Tell them what you are seeing/sensing.	You must interpret what you see so they will not misinterpret it based on their understanding of symbols.
You can lay your hands on them with permission.	You must get permission to touch them.

Believers	Others
Pray openly and freely.	Pray briefly with your eyes open.

You will also do better by avoiding King James-style flowery language when you prophesy.

One last tip: "The lost" do not like to be called lost. Using this language is politically incorrect and emotionally insensitive to people. Let's just call them "people" or people in need of God's love.

Getting Outside the Box

Let me explain why I am bringing such a radical message to you. God is calling us to step up and be ready, not only with revelation, but with practical application. We need to use the gift of wisdom and help people understand what God is saying. This involves getting outside the box of Christianity.

Let's look at Joseph, the dream interpreter. In Genesis 40, Joseph interpreted the dreams of Pharaoh's baker and cupbearer who were in prison with him:

> *When Joseph came to them the next morning, he saw that they were dejected. So he asked Pharaoh's officials who were in custody with him in his master's house, "Why do you look so sad today?" "We both had dreams," they answered, "but there is no one to interpret them." Then Joseph said to them, "Do not interpretations belong to God? Tell me your dreams"* (Genesis 40:6–8).

It is very interesting to note that they had dreams, but there was *"no one to interpret them"*—yet in Egypt there was no shortage of dream interpreters. What they were actually saying was that no one had been able to *interpret them correctly*. This is usually an indicator that the dream was from God.

Notice also that they were sad and dejected. This is symbolic of people everywhere today with dreams and callings from God. They are sad and depressed because there is no one to help them interpret what God is saying. We really are sitting on a gold mine of encounters, but it requires someone with the Spirit of God to interpret a dream from God.

> *The person without the Spirit does not accept the things that come from the Spirit of God but considers them foolishness, and **cannot understand** them because they are discerned only through the Spirit* (1 Corinthians 2:14).

Did you catch that? Only those with the Holy Spirit can understand and interpret things from God. As Joseph said, *"Do not interpretations belong to the Lord? Tell me your dreams"* (Genesis 40:8). We can apply this to prophetic words, tattoos, body art, life dreams, and night dreams.

I wish you could see what I have seen after interpreting thousands of dreams and tattoos to help people with their life goals and destiny. People are so hungry for the supernatural! They do not want a sermon or Bible verses, but most people open right up when they feel loved, accepted, cared for, and are being encouraged.

In the next chapter, I go into detail about how to have divine encounters with people. But first I want to give you a strategy that I have been using for a number of years. Once you get into an encounter and you have a person's attention, what do you do next?

MASH Units for God

During the Korean War, *MASH* units (Mobile Army Surgical Hospitals) were set up behind the front lines to attend to those wounded in battle. They did not have all the equipment needed to perform surgeries, but they saved many lives.

We need to become spiritual MASH units! I want to deputize you right now as an individual MASH unit to go into enemy territory and be a healer. Help pick up the wounded and restore them with hope and the power of love.

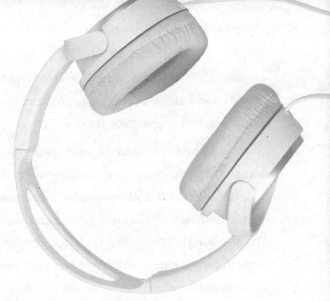

CHAPTER 10

Creative Ways of Hearing God

God's Voice Is All Around Us

God is speaking to you all the time. The more you understand His hidden voice, the better you will know your God-given destiny. In this chapter, we will look at various ways God speaks to us. This chapter is designed to awaken your God-given creative spirit, and look at how He can speak through just about anything.

Most of us are not aware that many things are ringing out with prophetic messages and deeper insight from God, be they movies, music, dreams, or even tattoos and piercings. If God can speak through Balaam's donkey then He can also speak to people through the symbolism of their body art. I will say upfront that I don't have any tattoos and I am not for or against them, but what I've noticed is that about a billion people have tattoos.

For a number of years, I have been interpreting the symbolism in tattoos using the same understanding of dreams. It might sound strange to some at first, but I've been seeing an amazing response when we help people understand that God may be speaking to them not only in their dreams but also through the design they chose for the tattoo or the type of piercing that they have. It is best to not judge things that you don't understand.

The options of how God can speak to us are endless because God has no limits and He loves everyone. Do not be put off from the topic of creativity if you feel that you are not creative. The fact is, we are all creative. God created the heavens and the earth, and we were created in His image (Genesis 1:27). That means we all have a built-in desire to create.

Creativity is not just for artists, musicians, dancers, and designers. You can be creative as a bookkeeper, banker, stay-at-home mom, programmer, attorney, or any other type of work. We can all be creative because God has given us a creative spirit. God is limitless, so what you can do through His love, power, and strength has no limits as well!

God loves you and desires for you to succeed and prosper. The more you know God as a loving Father, the better you will hear His voice. He is not mad at you, as many people portray Him to be. God is full of mercy and wants to see you succeed. The Holy Spirit is in you, and you have access to all that you need to get a breakthrough and help others do the same!

It is time to jump-start your creative flow and open your ability to hear the voice of God in all the areas of your life. People everywhere are trying to express themselves. What you might not realize is that there are prophetic messages behind a lot of these creative expressions, like ringtones, clothing, jewelry, music, and bumper stickers. We are all giving each other clues about what we value, which helps us connect with our true selves and God.

Most people do not have eyes to see that these things are important for hearing the voice of God. I started noticing them years ago. Now I use this revelation to help people discover clues about their destiny and how God is speaking to them through their choices of creative expression.

How I Discovered My Creativity

Until I was in my late thirties, I played my guitar every day, mostly by myself. I only wanted to do God's will, so I spent nearly all my time soaking in prayer and worshiping. I was so afraid of public speaking that I would not go to Bible studies if I knew I had to read aloud. I really thought my calling was to pray and intercede, and not have to deal with the outside world.

I had excuses that I thought confirmed these things. *I'm too shy and uneducated. I have ADD and dyslexia* (though I have had a lot of healing). *I tried, but never made it to Bible college.* I really believed God was speaking to me to isolate myself and not trust anyone. The problem was that I was doing it out of fear and emotional wounding from my past. The praying and worshiping I was doing in isolation were good, but not God's ultimate plan for me.

Now I intentionally make myself connect with people. I am a public speaker, but since I still do not like to read out loud, I memorize a lot and speak my messages clothed in stand-up comedy. This aids me with my inabilities and helps people connect with God. I am also a writer, even though I still do not spell very well. So, I use a spell checker and have a writing team that helps me.

I interact with tens of thousands of people every year, yet I am still an introvert by nature. I go back to my hotel room after events and get my introvert fix by journaling and hearing God. I still have never attended Bible college, but now my books are being used in Bible colleges. I was even approved by a seminary to supervise a Master of Divinity intern. I am crediting God for all of this.

Had I not discovered my full potential, I would have seriously limited myself. I would also have missed my higher calling of helping millions of people all over the world. Listen to me: There are so many people who are suffering from the same things you just read about me. The enemy may have wounded you, and like many people, you are thinking it is God's call to spend the majority of your time in the prayer room, isolated in intimacy, and not impacting the world.

I hope and pray I did not offend you. I am not saying to stop praying and spending time in intimacy. But there is no New Testament, biblical example of this becoming a ministry. I am still a prophetic intercessor and I spend two hours a day praying. But we *must* reach out to others. God wants to use you to change the world, but Satan wants you to believe that you are too shy or not smart enough. God created you to make a difference.

Do you want to make a positive, lasting impact on others? Sharing what God speaks to you should open people up to hear from God and not close them off. God wants you to have a life that gets you excited about getting up in the morning. You can do this in your current job or situation.

God wants to give you the desires of your heart. As your heart comes in line with His, He can trust you and give you things you love. God wants you to have passion for what you do and to *"work at [your job] with all your heart, as working for the Lord, not for human masters"*

(Colossians 3:23). This will change the spiritual atmosphere over you, and allow God's creative power to flow through all of your life.

For the longest time, I was stuck in a career that did not suit my personality or gifting. For nearly twenty years, I worked in the banking and finance industries in bill collections and credit management. I felt quite stifled most of the time because I did not know how to make a living any other way based on my education and experience.

Looking back over my life, at one time I was writing a new song every week, painting, taking long walks in nature, and playing guitar in a band. But my creativity seemed to vanish with the busyness of life. So I went on a journey to awaken God's creative gifts within me.

Keep in mind that there are no limits to how God can flow through you. When He begins to do something new, quite often we have to give up our old ways of thinking and doing things.

> *Forget the former things; do not dwell on the past. See, I am doing a new thing! Now it springs up; do you not perceive it? I am making a way in the wilderness and streams in the wasteland* (Isaiah 43:18–19).

It is really important to not dwell on the past. God wants to do something new and creative in your life right now.

Barbecue for the Homeless

At the age of thirty-five I left my corporate job to pursue ministry training. Going from a good paying management career in San Francisco to a minimum wage church internship was a shock. I was so hungry to do ministry that I was willing to do about anything. I was an intern for a year before realizing it was not my ultimate calling. I almost went bankrupt that year.

But I learned a lot during that internship. When I was in charge of local missions and outreach, we found out that the major food distribution programs in our county were closed on the weekends. So several churches got together and created a program called *SOS: Sandwiches on Sunday*. We would make over two hundred bag lunches and deliver them to the parking lot of the closed community center. People from the neighborhood would flock in to get the bag lunches we were handing out, and we would be on our way within minutes.

Then we got a creative thought from Heaven: Why not offer a barbecue for the needy? When it was time for our sandwich outreach, instead of peanut butter and jelly sandwiches, we brought barbecue grills and made hamburgers and hotdogs and other really good picnic food. We even brought in a band, and the neighborhood would flock in.

The people were so grateful that it shifted the spiritual atmosphere over our city and over us. We were able to see that these people in need had real lives, and we were able to bless them. We had so much favor that a secular band heard about what we did. They came in and shot a music video that was shown on MTV for the song, *We Want a Better Life*.

Creative Strategy to Start a Business

After suffering terribly financially that year, a businessman at my church helped me. I went on from that low-paying internship and started a computer networking business in the San Francisco Bay Area. It was not a fun time for me at all, but I knew God was in it.

How is running a computer business being creative? Even though it was a very left-brain time of my life, God gave me creative technical solutions during my prayer times that no one else could figure out, and I would get paid well for it.

In the 1990s, during the early rise of online home loan websites, I discovered a patch to get a mortgage loan processing software to run on wide-area networks and interact with the internet. It might not sound all that creative, but it was a strategy from Heaven that blessed us financially during a transition time in life. Honestly, I tried to give the solution away for free, but companies wanted to pay me to come in and install it on their systems.

Creative Computer Fix

During this time of interacting with all types of people in their cubicles and offices while fixing their systems, the Holy Spirit would speak to me and give me prophetic words for them. My office was in the San Francisco Bay area, but I landed a great client in Dallas, Texas. So, when giving prophetic words, I had to learn to communicate with people in San Francisco, who were mostly gay, liberal, and hostile to Christianity, and also in Dallas, who were very religious and not very open to the gifts of the Holy Spirit.

This was in the mid-to-late 1990s, before prophetic outreach was discovered in the United States. I had several years of intense, on-the-job training that later formed into creative prophetic outreach strategies.

It was five years of really hard work, but I got paid four times the amount of my corporate job and it freed my time up to pursue ministry training. The Lord gave me the strategy to get paid well as a consultant while I was growing and getting on-the-job training in prophesying to people in the marketplace. This was the best ministry training I could have ever gotten.

In 2001, I was one of the forerunners birthing the new movement of prophetic evangelism. I traveled extensively for seven years training people, launching dream interpretation and prophetic outreach teams. Our teams would go into New Age events, Mardi Gras, the Sundance Film Festival, and Burning Man (the largest pagan festival on earth).

This all came from a creative strategy from Heaven that was given to a frustrated bill collector living in San Francisco, crying out to God to be used. It sounds like I knew what I was doing and had a plan; but in reality, what I am sharing with you is all hindsight. I had no idea that this creative strategy was going to radically change the way we interact with people using the prophetic gifts. God created a new normal for how we can use the gifts.

I went on to sell that computer business, and we used the funds to plant several churches and launch outreach teams all around the world. I wrote several books, developed lots of training, and created a workshop that is still being taught today. With that groundwork in mind, let me share with you more about how we all can be creative.

God's Voice in Culture and the Arts

There are so many ways to express our creativity through art, writing, inventions, ideas, problem solving and music—the possibilities are endless. Jesus taught deep spiritual insights about the Kingdom of God through symbolic stories called parables. Many movies, songs, and various art forms have hidden messages and are essentially modern-day parables. The best way I can help you awaken to God's creative spirit is to activate your spiritual *"eyes to see and ears to hear."* To do that, I want to show you some creative ways that God speaks prophetically.

I first discovered this during my early computer business experiences. While sitting at a person's desk fixing the computer, God would speak to me through their pictures or items they had in their office. I had no idea it was even okay to do this. No one had trained me on it. In fact, the people leading prophetic ministry at my church at the time taught us to only say what God is saying to you—like a prophetic download—and to not look at natural things. Well, I guess I had not read my book or taken my course yet, because God would speak to me through prophetic messages in art, music, and movies to receive some of the solutions and strategies I just shared with you.

To get creativity flowing in your ability to see and hear God, let me describe some metaphoric messages in modern-day movies.

Superhero Movies

Most superhero movies have the same theme—supernaturally gifted people use their powers to help people and fight evil, and when they stop using their supernatural abilities, crime increases. This is symbolic of when Christians stop using their God-given supernatural gifts and evil appears to increase. But just like in the movies, when they go back to using their supernatural powers, the world seems to balance out again. God is calling us to use our spiritual gifts outside the church.

Spiderman

Spiderman was originally a comic book character, but there were three *Spiderman* movies that were remade and became popular in recent years. Spiderman was an everyday guy named Peter Parker. A spider that was used for a scientific experiment bit him, and he was infused with superpowers useful for fighting crime and restoring justice.

Spiders may seem evil, but Spiderman is not. This is symbolic of the many conservative Christians who believe Spirit-filled Christians are evil. Another very prophetic message—his name was Peter (who, in the Bible, was used to establish the Church) and he lived next door and was in love with Mary (who could represent the Church). But she was in love with the evil guy next door! This represents the Church being in love with the world or things that are not good for her.

In *Spiderman 2*, Peter did not realize who he was or the power he had. At one point, he had to start wearing glasses because he lost his supernatural ability to have "eyes that see." This represents the fact that we can lose our identity and spiritual eyesight. In Spiderman 3, Peter got black stuff on him (pride), and had to go to a church to get rid of it. These are not "Christian" movies, but they sure have a lot of prophetic significance!

The Incredibles

Another example helpful to understanding metaphors is the animated movie *The Incredibles*, about a family with supernatural powers. I want to give credit to Jeannine Rodriguez for this revelation that I have built on and used to train people all over the world.

The Parr family had five members, which is symbolic of the fivefold ministry gifts that are mentioned in the Bible (Ephesians 4:11).

The father had supernatural strength, but he was too strong and would break things. This is symbolic of people who become too spiritual and rigid, and lack love and grace. They inadvertently end up breaking a lot of things and hurting people around them. The dad needed balance, and he had that in his wife. Her supernatural power was flexibility. Strength requires flexibility, or we end up hurting people.

Most people thought that the daughter's supernatural gifting was the ability to disappear, but Violet wanted to disappear because she did not want to be seen. Later, she discovered that her true supernatural ability was to cover her family with a bubble of protection—a force field. This is symbolic of having the gift of prayer and intercession. When she discovered her true gift, she no longer wanted to disappear. Instead, she became very interactive with her friends.

Wanting to disappear is prophetic for people who are supernaturally gifted by God, but do not want anyone to know about it. This is called false humility, and there are many "Violets" out there who need to discover their true identity in God.

There was their son, Dash, whose ability was to move very quickly. This is symbolic of our need to move quickly in making decisions and getting things done.

Then there was the baby, Jack-Jack. Most people thought that Jack-Jack might have been evil because of his appearance, but he could do everything that all the other family members could do, all at once. He was the most gifted in the entire family, yet he was just an infant. This is symbolic of a generation that is rising up right now that is so very talented but not yet mature in their gifts and callings.

Another character in *The Incredibles* is the family friend, Buddy. He is not a family member, but he came to Mr. Parr and asked to be mentored. The dad had no time for him and told him to beat it, so Buddy went off on his own and built a machine that allowed him to do "supernatural things." It was a counterfeit of an actual supernatural gift, and is symbolic of people who have come to the Church to be trained in the things of God, but were sent away because they did not fit into the Church's family mold.

Many of these highly gifted people (like me in my past) were turned away because they were not understood. They went off discouraged, never to come near God or a church again. Some of them were so gifted that they developed or joined groups such as the Human Potential Movement and New Age. Many of them grew up in church or were pastor's kids. They are using biblical principles without a personal relationship with God or the power of the Holy Spirit.

I am not being judgmental here. I was once one of those highly gifted people who came to the church, but was turned away. I was even sent a letter from a church turning me over to Satan in hopes that my soul would be saved. This was very painful for me and took me away from my destiny for many years. Eventually, I did find my way back to the Lord, but it was a long journey that could have been avoided had Christians been more loving and accepting.

No Limits

But with God all things are possible (Matthew 19:26).

I want to encourage you to not limit how God can speak to you. I have only mentioned a few ways. God is speaking all the time but as Job says, we often do not perceive it (Job 33:14). God is opening up new revelation and understanding for us during what might seem like a challenging and difficult time on the earth. Ask the Lord to speak to you each day and get ready to receive!

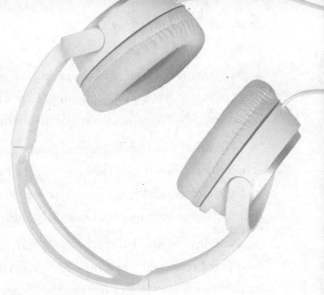

CHAPTER 11

Hearing God for Your Destiny

Angelic Encounter

In 2004 I lived in Los Angeles, the City of Angels. I had been doing prophetic outreaches for a few years and we were giving prophetic words of destiny to people. My concern was that many people I was training, including Christians, did not know their *own* destinies. You cannot give away what you do not have yourself. You can do it by faith for a while, but eventually you need to know God's will for your life. So I was crying out for a strategy.

I was awakened in the middle of the night by something brushing against my ear. I looked up and literally saw a beautiful glowing golden angel hovering over me and whispering into my ear. It was not a dream or a vision—it was really happening. Even though the encounter only lasted seconds, I remember every detail about it.

The angel was translucent and floating in midair just over my bed. It had golden skin, wore a flowing, bright white gown with gold weaved into the sleeves, and had a golden sash around its waist. As it hovered over me, it was holding back beautiful golden braids of hair.

Needless to say, I did what any man of God would do in that moment: I screamed like a little girl! My wife woke up, and the angel quickly swirled down to a light in the corner of our bedroom. Though she did not see the angel, she knew it was there and we both felt a thick presence of God filling the room. My wife asked what the angel had told me, but I could not remember.

I realize that once I write this, the encounter may not seem as powerful to you. I can almost hear you saying, "You don't remember what the angel said?" But I knew the spiritual principle from Job 33—sometimes God will seal things away, and our natural mind does not need to know it.

Sure enough, I began getting dreams and a lot of revelation after that experience. God bypassed my natural mind and gave me direct downloads from Heaven. I needed to "ask, seek, and knock" to pull it into the reality of my life.

This was a turning point in my life and ministry, and it led to my writing material on how people can find their destinies. The angel's message was an answer to the cry of my heart to "do something about the condition of things." Like many encounters from God, it took time to understand. I spent more than 1,500 hours researching and studying how to bring change to your life and discover your destiny, starting with myself! As I share with you what I discovered, my prayer is that it will radically change your life as well.

I had a vision of people who were obese and bloated with too many prophetic words and not enough action. They had tiny little legs, and had fallen over and could not get up. Many people today are in this condition—prophetic hopelessness—and it is one of the reasons why *"Hope deferred makes the heart sick, but a longing fulfilled is a tree of life"* (Proverbs 13:12). We need more than believing and hoping—we need a longing fulfilled!

God desires to bring about the prophetic words in our lives, but most people are waiting for God to do it and are not taking any steps toward receiving it.

People Want More

People everywhere want to know that their lives have more purpose than going to work, coming home, cooking, going to church, and hanging out watching movies on the weekends. There is nothing wrong with these things, but most people want more from life than just making a living. Life was meant to be lived with purpose, and we were all designed by God to have passion for living.

In reality, the decisions we make every day can change our lives. Yes, I know that ultimately God's love and power are what change us. But even so, we have to make a decision to receive them.

When you learn to make the right decisions or choices for the right reasons at the right time, your life will begin to change. If you do this consistently, you will begin to break through things that have held you back in the past. Procrastination is a more serious destiny-killer than you may realize. It is a plan of the enemy to rob us!

Getting spiritual people to take positive action in their lives is not an easy task, because spirituality and a relationship with God are not easily measured. Quite often, Christians can justify why they are stuck or have not moved forward. They claim that they do not feel "released by God" or they are not "gifted" or "called." Many will say, "I'll pray about it," which usually means, "No way." Though it is true that some people are waiting on the Lord and things have not been released to them yet.

Have you ever felt like something is holding you back from moving into a greater level of fulfillment or going forward in seeing your life dreams come true? The following are symptoms that you need a breakthrough:

- You want to do something positive, but do not know exactly where to start.

- You feel stuck in your current job, relationship, or situation.

- You feel like there is something more for you to do, but you do not know the details of what it is.

- You have difficulty making decisions or are afraid to make a wrong decision, so you do not decide at all.

- You procrastinate on a regular basis, even on things that are important for you to do.

- You have given up on some dreams or are less passionate than you once were.

- You have gifts and talents that you rarely use.

- You feel paralyzed to move forward.

- You often have negative thoughts about yourself.

- You are waiting for the perfect situation before you begin to pursue your dreams or destiny.

- You are not taking any initiative of your own, waiting for God to open doors of opportunity for you.

This is not meant to make you feel bad about yourself. In fact, these are all major signs that you have something greater to fulfill in life, and the enemy wants to stop you. After running study groups, I noticed that people who had a high destiny on their life seemed to be attacked in the area of their strength or calling. You need a breakthrough, and what I am about to share with you will help.

God is limitless. What you can do through His love and power has no limits. You can create a better spiritual life, career, relationships, physical health, and emotional stability. I want to show you some of the biblical principles that I discovered. If you combine them with a relationship with God and the empowerment of the Holy Spirit, you can accelerate into your life's purpose much more quickly than you ever dreamed possible. In the process, you will discover the supernatural life that God intended for you.

Easy as Connecting the Dots

Your life purpose or destiny is like a connect-the-dots drawing. It might not be clear now, but trust that God will guide you through the process. I have seen so many breakthroughs: people are losing weight, getting new jobs, finding their spiritual gifts, writing books, starting businesses, and producing new art and music, to name just a few.

What does all this have to do with finding your destiny? If you take small steps consistently over time, you will be prepared for the bigger life callings. Today I am able to write a full-sized book in less than three weeks because I write regularly and the content is ready when I am. It becomes easy to pull things together when you prepare yourself.

Many people live a life of avoidance and procrastination, waiting for God to speak to them and drop a sign from Heaven. In most cases, God has already given us all that we need to move forward in our destiny. Even if things do not seem clear right now, hearing God's voice and taking practical steps will help bring the clarity you need.

I have received feedback from many other people who have made radical changes in their lives as well. If you have not picked up on them yet, I have been sharing the following biblical principles with you throughout this book:

- All things are possible for those who believe.

- God is the Giver of good gifts.

- God is a loving Father who wants to give you good things.

- God is for you, and not against you or mad at you.

- God is not causing the bad things we see happening in the world.

- God wants to give you the desires of your heart, and He can do this as your heart and intentions become more like His.

- God wants to give you hope and a future, and to see you prosper and succeed.

- You are truly a new creation in Christ. The old things no longer have power over you unless you allow them to.

I want to be clear—life is *not* about achievement, it is about love and relationships.

But when you change the *quality* of your daily life, you feel better and are more likely to love people and connect with God on a deeper level. When you change your own life, you cannot help but change the lives of those around you. We must start with ourselves, because we cannot give away what we do not have within us.

Did you know that you are unique, and you are uniquely called and created by God to do something great? No one else can do what you can do.

"For I know the plans I have for you," declares the Lord, "plans to prosper you and not to harm you, plans to give you hope and a future" (Jeremiah 29:11).

We are all born with a high calling, but we tend to fall back down to a level of what we believe is possible. It really comes back to our beliefs—what we believe about ourselves, God, and the world around us. This falling back is usually powered by a negative view of ourselves and our view of God.

Seeing Ourselves as God Sees Us

All things really are possible for those who believe—and who take some steps toward what they feel called to do. We all have the potential for a high calling, which always requires time and effort to develop. Sadly, most people give up during the training and testing process.

Quite often we are not able to see our purpose and destiny, so we are required to rely on faith. *"Now faith is confidence in what we hope for and assurance of what we do not see"* (Hebrews 11:1). We need to live this principle of faith, and be certain of God's intentions for us, even though we may not see them yet.

Do not conform to the pattern of this world, but be transformed by the renewing of your mind. Then you will be able to test and approve what God's will is—his good, pleasing and perfect will (Romans 12:2).

Renewing your mind involves replacing your old mindset with a new one. Your new mindset is who you are becoming, not who you are or were. The Bible compares this transformation to stepping away from the picture of your old self and putting on a picture of your new self.

God sees us as who we are becoming, or in our full potential. For example, in Judges 6, Gideon is hiding in fear, and an angel comes and calls him a mighty man of valor. God treated Gideon the way He saw him in the future. And in John 1:40–42, Simon had just met Jesus. Even though Peter was still flaky, Jesus told him, *"You shall be called Peter,"* which means, "rock." Jesus treated Peter the way He saw him in the future, not how he was at that moment.

The key is to begin seeing yourself in your full potential in God. See yourself as God sees you, not as you once were or even as you are now, but by faith get a picture of who you are becoming in God. As you begin to live in this new mindset, it will not take long to become reality.

Destiny and Life Purpose

I use the words *destiny* and *life purpose* interchangeably because they actually are very similar. Your life purpose is the unique assignment from God that involves the development of your spiritual gifts and growing in godly character and love. Your life purpose is to grow in all that God has for you. When you do this, you will ultimately make the world a better place. This might sound like a cliché, but it is not. We really need to change the spiritual atmosphere around us, which can ultimately change the world!

Destiny is the direction you take your life, whether good or bad. Do not worry if it is not clear yet because it takes time to unfold. Remember that destiny is like a connect-the-dots drawing; each dot is an experience, season, or life lesson. The picture might not be clear right now, but it will become more clear as you "connect the dots" in your life.

God will sometimes accelerate things, and other times things slow down to a frustrating pace. This is all part of advancing through your stages of maturity. The important thing is to understand who God really is, who you are, and who you are becoming in God.

Do not give up! Hearing the voice of God is very important in the process of understanding your life purpose and destiny. Many of your night dreams point toward your life dreams. God has been giving you clues all your life about your purpose and destiny. Many of these clues lie in the things that you are gifted with or drawn to. This is not saying that everything you like is God's ultimate will for you, but He is the Giver of good gifts. The better you know Him and understand His heart, the more He can trust you with greater things.

Your destiny and life purpose are more about who you will become, and not necessarily what you do. Ultimately, everyone's destiny and life purpose are rooted in three of Jesus' messages.

Early on, Jesus said to Peter and Andrew, *"Come, follow me ... and I will send you out to fish for people"* (Matthew 4:19). First things first—follow Jesus and learn from Him. They were already fishermen, so it is not like He was telling them to become rabbis or something they were not wired for. The lesson here is that God wants to use your natural talents and gifts.

The second message from Jesus: *"Love the Lord your God with all your heart and with all your soul and with all your mind. ... Love your neighbor as yourself"* (Matthew 22:37, 39). In these verses, we see three loves: love God, love other people, and love ourselves. Most people focus only on loving God and forget that we need to love others and ourselves.

The last message is, *"Therefore go and make disciples ... teaching them to obey everything I have commanded [taught] you ..."* (Matthew 28:19-20). If you have learned anything from God in your life, you can share it with others. This is not just sharing the gospel message or Bible verses. If you have made it through tough times, share your story with others.

Biblical Principles of Change

> But seek first his kingdom and his righteousness, and all
> these things will be given to you as well (Matthew 6:33).

If you place a high value on your spiritual life and on building a relationship with God, He will guide you through all areas of your life. When I quoted Matthew 6:33, you may have been thinking, *Oh, I believe that.* But are you actually seeking the Kingdom every day?

We can know the truth of the Bible, but if we are not actually doing it, then we are lacking a tangible revelation of the truth. Once we get a revelation of any verse or principle, it becomes alive in us and gives us a spiritual push forward. If we take the revelation a step further, and we do something to practically use it or apply it in our life, then we begin to advance. If we do it regularly and make a habit or lifestyle from it, then momentum kicks in and we go to an entirely new level that few people are aware even exists.

There are many principles in the Bible that will unlock and open the doors to your future. You are probably already aware of these, but when you respond to them consistently, your life will change.

Dream Thief

> The thief comes only to steal and kill and destroy; I have
> come that they may have life, and have it to the full
> (John 10:10).

We all need a greater purpose in life and to be part of something that is bigger than ourselves. Have you ever felt like something is holding you back from achieving your life dreams? There is a dream thief that can try to take away your passions. We were all designed to have passion for living and to live life with purpose.

Ultimately, receiving God's love and power is what will change you the most. But even still, there are many people who have done this, yet remain unfulfilled and adrift.

Even Better than a Bucket List

Take some time to pray and ask God to show you things about your greater purpose and life calling. God wants to give you the desires of your heart, and this becomes easier as your heart comes in line with His.

Remember Psalm 37:4 says, *"Take delight in the Lord, and he will give you the desires of your heart."* If you have not done so already, make a "desires of your heart list." This is even better than a bucket list! These are the things that you would like to do and would bring you the greatest joy. It does not mean that you have to accomplish them all, but it is a good place to start.

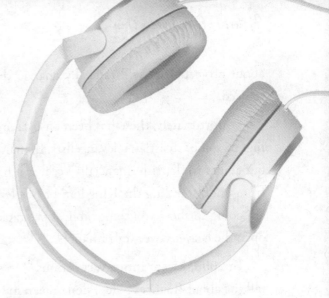

CHAPTER 12

Hearing God for Finances and Businesses

Throughout this book I have been activating your spiritual gifts and your ability to hear God every day. You are developing eyes to see and ears to hear and you are learning to discern. I have been activating dreams and creativity, your life purpose and your destiny.

Financial Healing

It is crucial to understand what God is saying right now regarding finances. For churches and ministries, our traditional donation model might not get us to the financial level that God wants for us over the next few years. We are being called to change the world, and with all the tragedies and disasters occurring, we need an abundance of resources. Because of this, God is releasing Kingdom financial strategies to bring about projects that will radically change the world and help people in need.

Unfortunately, there has been an overemphasis on financial offerings by some Christian televangelists. In many cases, this has weakened our ability to flourish financially because it has turned many people off from understanding the Kingdom principle of giving and receiving. I am going to show you some biblical principles and strategies that can open the heavens over your finances.

In 2008, I went into a very serious "Job season." Even though I'm talking about finances here, I don't mean my *job*, I mean suffering like Job! Nothing would work financially and my ministry went $50,000 in debt, but I knew that God's ways and His Word had not changed. I applied the biblical principles of giving and receiving, sowing and reaping, and seeking first the Kingdom of God. Even though I was in a terrible time of obscurity, I kept on ministering to others. That same year, God began to use me to prophesy strategies into ministries and businesses. I prophesied a strategy to a businessman from South Africa that netted him $1 million within eight months.

In 2009, he had me come speak at a conference in Cape Town, South Africa. The week I was there, I had several major angelic encounters in my hotel and during the meetings. In one especially significant experience, an angel came into my hotel room just before I was leaving to go speak that night. I began writing the verses and strategies as I heard them. I usually see or hear things that I have to interpret, but this was a true "prophetic download." I normally do not get dictations from Heaven like that.

As I gave the message that night, many people were set free in the area of finances. We had been praying for a financial blessing for our ministry, and we received it! We also heard stories about miracles that happened during and following the meeting.

I am not talking about a "wealth and prosperity" or a "name it and claim it" message. In fact, prosperity for us should not be about a certain quantity of money, but is simply having the freedom and means to do what God calls us do, when He calls us to do it. Financial blessing creates a lifestyle that frees your time to focus on ministry and attend to the things God reveals. True wealth and true riches are found in a relationship with God our Father, through Jesus Christ.

> *My goal is that they may be encouraged in heart and united in love, so that they may have the full riches of complete understanding, in order that they may know the mystery of God, namely, Christ, in whom are hidden all the treasures of wisdom and knowledge* (Colossians 2:2–3).

True wealth in the Kingdom of God is based on the principles of spiritual understanding, mysteries, and treasures of wisdom and knowledge. Wealth from a Kingdom standpoint is not measured by the size of your bank account, but on your ability to love and have God's heart.

Biblical Principles about Money

Money is not evil in and of itself: *"For the love of money is a root of all kinds of evil. Some people, eager for money, have wandered from the faith and pierced themselves with many griefs"* (1 Timothy 6:10). It is the *love of money* that is dangerous.

God owns everything! *"The earth is the Lord's, and everything in it, the world, and all who live in it"* (Psalm 24:1), and *"every animal of the forest is mine, and the cattle on a thousand hills"* (Psalm 50:10). Maybe we need a "cows for cash" intercession group, who will ask God to sell a cow and send some cash!

God will use money to test our motives and see if He can trust us with Kingdom wealth:

Whoever can be trusted with very little can also be trusted with much, and whoever is dishonest with very little will also be dishonest with much. So if you have not been trustworthy in handling worldly wealth, who will trust you with true riches? And if you have not been trustworthy with someone else's property, who will give you property of your own? (Luke 16:10–12)

You need to work at your job as if you are working for God:

Whatever you do, work at it with all your heart, as working for the Lord, not for human masters, since you know that you will receive an inheritance from the Lord as a reward. It is the Lord Christ you are serving (Colossians 3:23–24).

In many cases, God is waiting for us to view our current job as if we are working for Him before He will release us into something new. This was the case for me. In 1993, I was crying out to God, "When will You release me from my corporate job so I can do ministry full time?" I was already doing so much ministry after work and on the weekends. God spoke to me that He was not going to release me to full-time ministry until I understood Colossians 3:23 and used my spiritual gifts at work like I do at church. That was the turning point for me.

The downside of being prophetic is that we can get caught up in always battling for the future and forget to enjoy the present. But there is power in being content and grateful:

I know what it is to be in need, and I know what it is to have plenty. I have learned the secret of being content in any and every situation, whether well fed or hungry, whether living in plenty or in want. I can do all this through him who gives me strength (Philippians 4:12–13).

The early New Testament Church was known for giving even beyond its means. So go ahead and give extravagantly, because you will never out-give God!

> *Remember this: Whoever sows sparingly will also reap sparingly, and whoever sows generously will also reap generously* (2 Corinthians 9:6).

God Will Open Doors

> *Ask and it will be given to you; seek and you will find; knock and the door will be opened to you. For everyone who asks receives; the one who seeks finds; and to the one who knocks, the door will be opened* (Matthew 7:7–8).

I love using the acronym ASK (Ask, Seek, Knock) to remind myself of this verse and the insights it holds. Now let's take it deeper. As I mentioned, there is value in waiting on God. But sometimes when we are waiting on Him, He in fact is waiting on us to take some steps by faith! In Matthew 7:7–8, Jesus instructs us to knock and the door will be opened.

In Revelation 3:20, Jesus tells us to open the door because *He* is the one knocking: *"Here I am! I stand at the door and knock. If anyone hears my voice and opens the door, I will come in and eat with that person, and they with me."*

Oftentimes, God has already given us what we need to take the next step toward our destiny. Which door of opportunity is before you right now? Do you need to be proactive with what God is calling you to and take some steps? Or is God building your faith right now to hear His voice and open the door? You will always need a level of faith to do the new things God is calling you to do.

There are practical things we can all do regarding finances. Be wise and get advice, especially on big decisions. Learn to recognize God's voice; He will guide you and speak to you about your money. Learn to live within your means, use a budget or spending plan, pay off debt and develop savings. The goal is not to stop spending; if we all did that, people would lose their jobs! So continue to give and spend within reason.

Do not limit yourself to thinking only logically about money; let go of what you think is limiting you and get a heavenly strategy. This is not a chapter on how to get out of debt, though many people have after learning and applying financial principles in the Bible that most people miss.

I wrote a book, *How to Flip Your Financial Future,* that will help you apply these principles with strategies of how to get out of debt and start a business part time online—to help accelerate your way into what God is calling you to. We are truly living in a time of divine opportunities and God is waiting for people to ask and receive the strategy for financial breakthrough in your life.

God Wants to Bless Businesses

In Luke 5:1–11, Jesus got into Peter's boat and instructed him where to fish. They caught such a huge load that Peter called his business partners, James and John, to help bring it all in. They then sold those fish, and their business was blessed. Notice in verse 4 that they were in "deep water" or out of their comfort zone: *"When he had finished speaking, he said to Simon, 'Put out into deep water, and let down the nets for a catch.'"*

The lesson? Following instructions from God brings blessing. When Jesus told Peter to put out in deep water, Peter was already tired from fishing all night and frustrated because they had not caught anything. Still, he answered, *"But because you say so, I will let down the nets"*

(Luke 5:5). Jesus asked Peter to do something that did not make sense, but doing it anyway brought a huge return for Peter's business.

Another example from the Bible is the financial arrangement between Jacob and his father-in-law, Laban:

> But Laban said to [Jacob], "If I have found favor in your eyes, please stay. I have learned by divination that the Lord has blessed me because of you." He added, "Name your wages, and I will pay them" (Genesis 30:27–28).

Laban noticed that he was blessed when Jacob worked for him.

Jacob negotiated a deal to only take *"every speckled or spotted sheep, every dark-colored lamb and every spotted or speckled goat"* from Laban's flock as his wages (Genesis 30:32). It turns out that he was following an angel's instructions and did something that seemed illogical. Here is what Jacob told his wives as they traveled back to his homeland with a large flock of their own:

> In breeding season I once had a dream in which I looked up and saw that the male goats mating with the flock were streaked, speckled or spotted. The angel of God said to me in the dream, "Jacob," I answered, "Here I am." And he said, "Look up and see that all the male goats mating with the flock are streaked, speckled or spotted, for I have seen all that Laban has been doing to you" (Genesis 31:10–12).

God gave Jacob an unusual strategy to bless him and his family, in spite of Laban's attempts to take advantage of him and keep Jacob from his God-given destiny. In a similar way, God will use you to bless the place you work, and in turn your employer can bless you.

My Story

I was working for a company in San Francisco in the 1990s when God spoke to me about using my spiritual gifts at work as well as at church. The president of the company was a "Laban" style of leader. He was not godly, did not pay us for sick time, and was somewhat harsh.

One morning while in prayer, God directed me to pray and fast for the company and the company's finances. Later at work, I told the president what God showed me for the company. He pulled me into his office and asked with whom I had talked and what I knew. As it turned out, the company had run into a terrible importing problem that could prevent it from receiving the main products, which were manufactured overseas.

When I told him I was praying and fasting and God had spoken to me, tears came to his eyes. He started inviting me into meetings and would ask, "Doug, are you getting anything?" I had received several prophetic words, which I acted on that year. The company was blessed and we pulled through. He did not understand how I got the information, but he realized that my praying for his company seemed to change the atmosphere. When I left that job to go into ministry a few years later, they helped support me even more than my church did.

Supernatural Provision

Sometimes God will meet our needs in strange and unusual ways. For example, Jesus told Peter to pay their taxes by catching a fish and finding a coin in its mouth (Matthew 17:24–27). When God tells us to do something, it may not make sense in the natural realm. We need to get confirmation before taking action—especially for major decisions like changing jobs or moving to another place. In these cases, you will want multiple confirmations.

God can bless us even in an economic downturn. My wife and I made money on a house we sold during the 2008 housing downturn. God gave us a strategy to obtain the water rights for the land, which caused the land's value to go up $30,000 while the house itself decreased in value.

In Genesis 26, Isaac listened to God and got a strategy to reap a hundredfold during a major famine. Isaac's first response when the famine came was to go to Egypt, as his father Abraham had done previously. God spoke to Isaac and gave him a strategy to go into the land of the Philistines, who were his enemies, and make an agreement with an ungodly king. Because Isaac listened to God and followed a strategy, he was greatly blessed during the downturn.

Isaac planted crops in that land and the same year reaped a hundredfold, because the Lord blessed him (Genesis 26:12).

This is a prophetic word for today. Do not fear, but listen to God and He will give instructions and prophetic insight on how to be blessed during any economic downturn or tragedy on earth.

In Genesis 40, Joseph interpreted dreams for Pharaoh's baker and cupbearer while they were all in prison. That set him up to interpret two dreams for Pharaoh regarding seven years of plenty followed by seven years of famine (Genesis 41:28–36). Notice that Pharaoh was a world leader who was not a believer in Jehovah God.

Joseph went on to give Pharaoh advice on how to respond: Store up grain in the time of plenty and sell it to the world in the time of famine. This resulted in great blessing for Egypt. Also, Joseph was released from prison and promoted to second-in-command over all of Egypt. Even Joseph's family was saved from the famine and brought to Egypt. During a big famine and economic downturn, Israel received new clothes, houses, and gold!

God may very well have you in a "prison time," and He is keeping you on reserve to step up at the right time and the right place to release Kingdom strategies. God wants to use Josephs and Josephines in the business world to bless the Church and the Kingdom in the years to come.

The "Joseph Calling"

Similar to Joseph, God is setting up men and women to step on the scene and interpret dreams for leaders in business and government, or provide wisdom from God for a situation. I feel that I am one of them, and there are many people who will read this book who are as well. Like Joseph, we have been wrongly accused and mistreated, and it seems like God has forgotten us. Now is the time to prepare, because God is about to release the Josephs.

If you have this type of prophetic calling, chances are you have been rejected. The first step in preparation is to embrace your calling and get healed from any rejection you have experienced. Let go of unforgiveness, and do not let the losses of the past hinder you from moving forward. Realize that you are already in ministry training right now, so work in your job as if you are working for God. Joseph served under Potiphar, Pharaoh's servant, before he could serve as leader under Pharaoh. Do you recognize how God is training you right now?

In the 1980s and 1990s, I had three jobs where I worked as an assistant under an old management style. I had to honor the old management while introducing new technology and a management style that made the companies more effective and profitable. Today I am doing this very thing in the Church, honoring the old style while introducing the new.

Another step in developing the Joseph calling is learning to communicate. If we are called to influence the influencers of the world, we need to stop trying to convert everyone we meet. Instead, when we are full of God's love and power like Joseph, they will come to us. It is important to develop nonreligious language so people understand what God is trying to say to them through us.

Use your spiritual gifts right now—at your job, in your home, at school. Do not wait. What I am doing now is not all that different from 1993, when I prayed for the company I worked for and shared prophetic words with the president and in meetings. God wants to use you where you are right now!

Courtroom of Heaven

It helps to understand that some parts of Heaven work similarly to the court system on earth. I had a prophetic dream that I was praying about a legitimate complaint against a publisher that had gone out of business. My book got caught up in the process and was stuck—unable to be published. (This was happening in real life, and I was really upset about it.) In the dream, I began to pray and was taken by an angel to the courthouse of Heaven. It looked like a regular, giant courthouse, and it was jam-packed with Christians complaining and filing motions against other Christians. The place was chaotic, and the angels assigned to each case were running low on time and resources.

The angel standing next to me said that this is going on in the courtroom of Heaven every day. Many Christians are accusing other Christians and clogging up resources of Heaven. The angel asked me, "Would you be willing to settle your complaint out of court?" I was there to file a complaint also, but I said, "By all means, yes, I will settle out of court." Then I woke up.

A week later I had another dream, and the same angel was with me. It was a mediating angel, who sat down with the publisher and me to help us work it all out. A short time later, in the natural, my contract was returned to me without even contacting the company. It had been settled in Heaven and manifested on earth.

There is a process and procedure to follow when you take a complaint before God. Certain things have to happen, especially when you have a complaint against Christian brothers and sisters. Maybe this is why the apostle Paul said to not sue each other in court, and why God is giving us the spirit of reconciliation. Now I realize that when we mediate together over our disagreements, the outcome is a win-win situation. I am not saying that we should never go to court, but instead of accusing each other, we should try to settle our grievances quickly. Love overcomes and never fails.

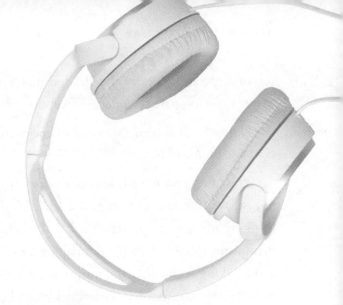

CHAPTER 13

Opening the Heavens Over You ⟳

If there is something you've been praying about and have not seen a breakthrough, there is a good chance you need a strategy from God. What I am going to share with you will work for getting a breakthrough wherever you need one.

There is nothing like going to work and doing things that do not feel like work because you are doing what you were created to do. I am living my dream right now, but I had to take steps to get here. In 2012, my ministry was still $30,000 in debt. We had worked hard to reduce it, but I had been on the road, doing over 150 meetings a year for ten years, faithfully doing what God had called me to do. I was doing everything I knew to do, but the old ways of doing things were no longer working. I was so desperate, I decided to sell a desk on Craigslist.com to get money to buy some software to update my website.

I knew I still needed a strategy, so I began decreeing the things that God had promised us.

The Lord gave me a financial strategy to pay off the debt of our ministry within just a few months. I had to get out of my old way of thinking and operating. Afterward, I developed a completely new way to minister online, which did not require me to be on the road traveling and speaking at churches and ministries. There is still a value and need for traveling ministry, but sometimes it can be harmful to our health and the well-being of our families.

From the proceeds of this new strategy, I was able to not only pay off the debt, but I was able to hire a company to update my website, I self-published a book, and relocated back to Los Angeles where God was calling me. Yes, God blessed us, but we also had to say yes to the plan and work very hard in the process. As a bonus, I did not have to sell my desk! We now operate our ministry debt-free and give to causes as God directs us.

Since that time, I have been able to be strategically located in the Hollywood area to pray and positively influence the arts and entertainment industries. My wife and I have truly given it all for the Kingdom of God and we have had our share of spiritual warfare, but the Lord has blessed us. Please hear my heart—this is not about money at all. It is about having the resources to fulfill our callings, as small or great as they might be.

Activation to Open the Heavens

In this book, I have written extensively about things that will close off your ability to hear God clearly. Whatever you focus on becomes your experience, whether it is based on reality or not. Most of us have been trained to look for things that are wrong instead of the good things that God has given us. A negative focus or outlook can cause us to easily miss the positive solution from Heaven.

Pride, unforgiveness, and false humility in our lives can cause us to not hear God clearly.

Being too logical can breed unbelief. Even Jesus was not able to perform miracles when there was a concentrated amount of logic and unbelief in an area.

There are ways to break through negativity, unbelief, and anything that gets between you and God. Realize that God is for you, and everything that happens to you is to help train and advance you. You can change your mindset to *"all things are possible"* and *"I can do all things through Christ who gives me strength."* Change the spiritual atmosphere around you by consistently sowing love, grace, gratitude, and generosity into the lives of others.

When you understand that God is greater than everything, you can adopt a *positive Kingdom lifestyle.* When you experience negative attacks, you can refocus and flip them into a positive outcome by releasing the opposite. Speak good things about people who say negative things about you. When you need a financial breakthrough, help someone else financially. If you need help with a situation, look for opportunities to help others with something they need. Practice the power of encouraging others. Good things will come back to you, and you will become unstoppable in finding and fulfilling your destiny in God.

In his first letter, John tells us that the Spirit within us is greater than the one in the world around us (1 John 4:4). We can change the spiritual atmosphere around us by loving, blessing, and being an encouragement everywhere we go. Remember that what you sow you will reap. If you sow grumbling, doubt, fear, depression, anxiety, and complaining, then that is what you will get in return. But if you sow blessing, love, and encouragement, your life will overflow with God's blessings.

The Power of Agreement

> *Again, truly I tell you that if two of you on earth agree about anything they ask for, it will be done for them by my Father in heaven. For where two or three gather in my name, there am I with them* (Matthew 18:19–20).

The ultimate activation to open the heavens—and keep them open over you—is agreeing with God to remove any judgments that you may have come into agreement with over yourself and others. There is power in agreeing with God's love and grace.

Let's look at how Jesus did this with the woman caught in adultery. When she was brought to Jesus, He saw that the condemnation and judgment of her sin was keeping her from her destiny of "true love." Jesus saw the work of the enemy and released God's love, which was the opposite of what she was experiencing in her life.

> *"In the Law Moses commanded us to stone such women. Now what do you say?" But Jesus bent down and started to write on the ground with his finger. When they kept on questioning him, he straightened up and said to them, "Let any one of you who is without sin be the first to throw a stone at her." Again he stooped down and wrote on the ground. At this, those who heard began to go away one at a time, the older ones first, until only Jesus was left, with the woman still standing there. Jesus straightened up and asked her, "Woman, where are they? Has no one condemned you?" "No one, sir," she said. "Then neither do I*

condemn you," Jesus declared. "Go now and leave your life of sin" (John 8:5–11).

When Jesus broke the "judgments" people had against her, it freed her up to change her life. Jesus waited until the condemning voices left before He spoke a tender word of grace and forgiveness to the woman. We need to also stand up for others in this way.

The Law of Moses commands condemnation, but the law of grace and love demands forgiveness. This applies to people who are using the Law of Moses to judge people in lifestyles or opinions they do not agree with. Judgments hold people down, but mercy, grace, and forgiveness free them up.

Love Not Judge

The Barna Group, a Christian research company, asked what words or phrases best describe Christianity. The top response among Americans ages 16–29 was "anti-homosexual." For a staggering *91 percent* of non-Christians, this was the first word that came to their minds when asked about the Christian faith. The same was true for 80 percent of young churchgoers.

The next most common descriptions of Christians were: judgmental, hypocritical, and too involved in politics. I wept when I heard these statistics. God forgive us for not demonstrating Your love and grace!

The spirit of accusation has been dominating the Church for the past few decades and making the body of Christ sick. We are living in a Church era where we have been so focused on sanctification, or being set apart and trying to be perfect, that a spirit of legalism and accusation has crept into the Church. We are back to trying to live by the rules of the Law instead of grace and love. Rules cause us to be judgmental toward those who do not follow them.

One of the names given to Satan is *"the accuser of our brothers and sisters"* (Revelation 12:10).

What I see the enemy doing over and over is influencing people to accuse each other. We need to be very careful to not accuse others, but build them up instead. When we accuse others, we are also holding ourselves down, because if we judge others we will be judged ourselves.

This is the condition of many people today, and the biggest reason people are not hearing the voice of God, getting healed, or receiving the financial breakthroughs they need. God is releasing a spirit of reconciliation to offset the strong, negative spirit of accusation. There are many Bible verses that talk about blessing people and not cursing them, such as:

> *Bless those who persecute you; bless and do not curse* (Romans 12:14).

> *Out of the same mouth come praise and cursing. My brothers and sisters, this should not be* (James 3:10).

Instead of accusing people, we need to love, not judge them:

> *The reason the Son of God appeared was to destroy the devil's work* (1 John 3:8).

> *All this is from God, who reconciled us to himself through Christ and gave us the ministry of reconciliation* (2 Corinthians 5:18).

Surprised by the Power of Love

I have extensively researched the Bible about love versus judgments. When we step out from under the grace that the blood of Jesus brought us, we get enslaved to rules and accusations.

There are benefits of love that can be seen in a person's life:

- Love conquers all
- Love overcomes
- Love never fails
- Love is patient and kind
- Love covers a multitude of sin

I say this in love to you—many people are displaying the opposite of the key benefits of love mentioned in 1 Corinthians 13.

- We are being overcome
- We are not patient
- Things seem to have failed
- Many people are battling a multitude of sins

The solution is to love. It will bring you into proper alignment with God, and allow heavenly blessings to flow to you.

Jesus' Two Greatest Commandments

Jesus replied: "Love the Lord your God with all your heart and with all your soul and with all your mind.' This is the first and greatest commandment. And the second is like it: 'Love your neighbor as yourself.' All the Law and the Prophets hang on these two commandments" (Matthew 22:37–40).

Love God, love your neighbor, and love yourself. We need to be careful that we are not only loving people we agree with, or who believe the same as do. We need to love people no matter who or what they represent or believe.

> *You have heard that it was said, "Love your neighbor and hate your enemy." But I tell you, love your enemies and pray for those who persecute you, that you may be children of your Father in heaven. He causes his sun to rise on the evil and the good, and sends rain on the righteous and the unrighteous. If you love those who love you, what reward will you get? Are not even the tax collectors doing that? And if you greet only your own people, what are you doing more than others? Do not even pagans do that?* (Matthew 5:43–47)

A seemingly forgotten and often misquoted verse is John 13:34–35: *"A new command I give you: Love one another. As I have loved you, so you must love one another. By this everyone will know that you are my disciples, if you love one another."* People will know we are followers of Christ by our love *for each other.* When we demonstrate to the world that we can agree among ourselves, we come into agreement with God—instead of the spirit of division.

We often read First Corinthians 13 at weddings and cry, only to walk away and forget what we heard:

> *If I have the gift of prophecy and can fathom all mysteries and all knowledge, and if I have a faith that can move mountains, but do not have love, I am nothing. If I give all I possess to the poor and give over my body to hardship that I may boast, but do not have love, I gain nothing* (1 Corinthians 13:2–3).

Do you know that if you do not love people unconditionally, you can stop financial blessings from coming into your life?

*Therefore, if you are offering your gift at the altar and there remember that your brother or sister has something against you, leave your gift there in front of the altar. **First go and be reconciled to them; then come and offer your gift.** Settle matters quickly with your adversary who is taking you to court. Do it while you are still together on the way, or your adversary may hand you over to the judge, and the judge may hand you over to the officer, and you may be thrown into prison. Truly I tell you, you will not get out until you have paid the last penny"* (Matthew 5:23–26).

Many people are in a prison of financial hardship because of accusations and disagreements with others. A verse that I have heard during offerings at churches and meetings is Luke 6:38. Let's read it in context of what Jesus was saying:

Do not judge, and you will not be judged. Do not condemn, and you will not be condemned. Forgive, and you will be forgiven. Give, and it will be given to you. A good measure, pressed down, shaken together and running over, will be poured into your lap. For with the measure you use, it will be measured to you (Luke 6:37–38).

Yes, this principle applies to money as well, but Jesus said it in context of forgiving others. If we extend forgiveness and grace to others, then we will have a blessing that will be poured into our laps. When I am asked to receive an offering at a meeting, I often walk people through forgiving others before they give. We have witnessed amazing breakthroughs as a result.

What about Righteous Anger?

> *Therefore each of you must put off falsehood and speak truthfully to your neighbor, for we are all members of one body. "In your anger do not sin": Do not let the sun go down while you are still angry, and do not give the devil a foothold* (Ephesians 4:25–27).

Most people use these verses to justify their cause and have forgotten the call God has given us to love and reconcile. Truth must be spoken in love. That is why Paul said when you get angry, do not sin. Remember that judging and accusing is sinning. Yes, there is such a thing as righteous anger, but when you cross over into hurting others instead of reconciling, you have given the devil a foothold in your life.

If you do not first examine your own life before trying to point out something in someone else's life, then you are being hypocritical. By looking at our own stuff first, we can get a clear vision:

> *Why do you look at the speck of sawdust in your brother's eye and pay no attention to the plank in your own eye? How can you say to your brother, "Brother, let me take the speck out of your eye," when you yourself fail to see the plank in your own eye? You hypocrite, first take the plank out of your eye, and then you will see clearly to remove the speck from your brother's eye* (Luke 6:41–42).

God is calling you into emotional and spiritual maturity. As you read the following passages from First Corinthians 13, let the words and meaning wash over your spirit:

> *Love is patient, love is kind. It does not envy, it does not boast, it is not proud. It does not dishonor others, it is not self-seeking, it is not easily angered, it keeps no record*

of wrongs. Love does not delight in evil but rejoices with the truth. It always protects, always trusts, always hopes, always perseveres. Love never fails ...

When I was a child, I talked like a child, I thought like a child, I reasoned like a child. When I became a man, I put the ways of childhood behind me. For now we see only a reflection as in a mirror; then we shall see face to face. Now I know in part; then I shall know fully, even as I am fully known. And now these three remain: **faith, hope and love. But the greatest of these is love** (1 Corinthians 13:4–8,11–13).

Self-Activation: Love, Not Judge

Begin by asking God to show you if there are people you have not forgiven. You do not have to agree with what they did to forgive them. Write down any names that come to mind.

Ask God to reveal if there are people groups that you are uncomfortable or angry with, or have not shown love and the spirit of reconciliation toward: people in different lifestyles, different faiths and beliefs, different political parties, etc. Write these down as they come to mind.

Next, ask God to forgive you for words you may have spoken over others that have cursed you, whether knowingly or unknowingly. Ask His forgiveness for judging others instead of loving them, for not extending mercy and love to others when you had the chance, and for unintentionally driving anyone away from God instead of drawing them closer.

Now take some time to watch and listen for God's response. Let His forgiveness soak deeply into your heart and spirit. Write down what

He says and shows to you, so you can go back and see how God works in your heart and life over time.

Invitation to More

As God opens the heavens over you once you have cleared the spiritual airways, you will experience God's love in ways you never dreamed possible. In the next few chapters we are going to explore the supernatural parts of God and the Bible. God is calling you to go deeper with Him.

Psalm 42:7–8 says, *"Deep calls to deep in the roar of your waterfalls; all your waves and breakers have swept over me. By day the Lord directs his love, at night his song is with me—a prayer to the God of my life."*

The Lord is calling you into greater intimacy and knowing His ways. The supernatural parts of God help take Him off the pages of the Bible and make it all reality!

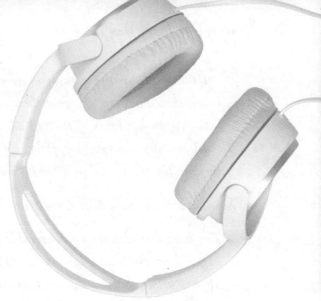

CHAPTER 14

God Speaks Supernaturally

Many Christians today have put God in a box and they only experience Him through reading the Bible or going to worship services. God is way bigger than that. We tend to focus on the healing miracles of Jesus Christ; but when I read the Bible, my eyes are continually opened to the awesome and sometimes strange occurrences.

We serve the God who cannot be explained. In the Bible, water parts, donkeys talk, thunder speaks, water turns to wine, angels perform prison breaks, and earthquakes open prison doors.

Jesus did some strange and supernatural things. One time, He disappeared as an angry mob tried to grab Him:

All the people in the synagogue were furious when they heard this. They got up, drove him out of the town, and took him to the brow of the hill on which the town was built, in order to throw him off the cliff. But he walked right through the crowd and went on his way (Luke 4:28–30).

Another time, Jesus walked on water and freaked out His friends:

The boat was already a considerable distance from land, buffeted by the waves because the wind was against it. Shortly before dawn Jesus went out to them, walking on the lake. When the disciples saw him walking on the lake, they were terrified. "It's a ghost," they said, and cried out in fear. But Jesus immediately said to them: "Take courage! It is I. Don't be afraid" (Matthew 14:24–27; also John 6:19–21 and Mark 6:47–49).

After He was raised from the dead, Jesus walked through a wall:

On the evening of that first day of the week, when the disciples were together, with the doors locked for fear of the Jewish leaders, Jesus came and stood among them and said, "Peace be with you!" (John 20:19; also Luke 24:33-39 and Mark 16:14)

Jesus could read people's minds:

Some men brought to him a paralyzed man, lying on a mat. When Jesus saw their faith, he said to the man, "Take heart, son; your sins are forgiven." At this, some of the teachers of the law said to themselves, "This fellow is blaspheming!" Knowing their thoughts, Jesus said, "Why do you entertain evil thoughts in your hearts?" (Matthew 9:2–4)

I have seen and experienced so many supernatural occurrences and miracles that I have lost count. I want you to know this amazing side of God, too. Jesus said, *"Very truly I tell you, whoever believes in me will do the works I have been doing, and they will do even greater things than these, because I am going to the Father"* (John 14:12).

Most of all, I want you to develop godly character, humility, and love so God can speak through you and use you powerfully: *"I keep asking that the God of our Lord Jesus Christ, the glorious Father, may give you the Spirit of wisdom and revelation, so that you may know him better"* (Ephesians 1:17).

What Is Stopping Us?

Ignorance and fear are the main reasons we do not have more supernatural encounters. Many evangelical seminaries teach *cessationism*—the idea that the gifts of the Holy Spirit ceased to operate after the death of the original twelve apostles. This has been made popular over the past hundred years or so, during the rise of modern thinking.

The increase of scientific knowledge and information has led to a focus on logic and reasoning instead of faith and believing. We have been conditioned to use our minds and not our spirits. Many Christians even take pride in trying to prove that supernatural things of God do not exist. If you tell someone about a supernatural thing God did, most people will not believe you.

A limited understanding of God can lead to unbelief, which prevents people from experiencing this side of God. Jesus could not do miracles in places that had a concentration of unbelief or lacked faith. Charismatic Christians tend to focus too much on the demonic and not enough on God's Holy Spirit and angels. I used to be one of them and I would see and hear demons as a result. It took a concerted effort to stop listening to them, since they are liars anyway.

Fear is another big reason that Christians shy away from the supernatural. Horror movies have caused many to grow up fearing supernatural experiences—good or bad. God showed me that nightmares, which often come after watching scary movies, are an attack of the enemy to get children to be fearful of the supernatural. Many grow up being afraid of seeing a ghost or even an angel. I had terrible nightmares and demonic attacks throughout my childhood, so I know that fear can stop you from seeing and experiencing the supernatural things of God.

Intimacy Brings Holiness

There has been a recent surge in teaching people that we must be holy to experience God. For years, this type of thinking kept me locked in a spin cycle of looking at negative things in my life as opposed to God's grace. Focusing too much on trying to become holy and avoiding sin can distract us from understanding God's grace and love for us. Do not get me wrong; we need to become more like Christ. But it is intimacy with God that will bring a desire to be holy, not the other way around.

We can begin to think that God is not visiting us because of our sin. While that is possible, my experience is that we will always have some level of sin to deal with in our lives. More often, it is because we are not actively looking for God that we do not experience Him, and have not developed spiritual *"eyes to see"* or our ability to discern.

My spiritual life radically changed the day I invited God into my daily life, messy or not. I had been a Christian for over ten years before I understood this. I found that when we focus on God's love and acceptance instead of focusing on missing the mark, we come into agreement with Heaven over our lives and move into a new level of authority.

When I understood this revelation, I gave up my legalistic views of being holy:

> *And [God] raised us up together, and made us sit together in the heavenly places in Christ Jesus, that in the ages to come He might show the exceeding **riches of His grace** in His kindness toward us in Christ Jesus. For by **grace** you have been saved through faith, and that not of yourselves; it **is the gift of God**, not of works, lest anyone should boast* (Ephesians 2:6–9 NKJV).

We need *"eyes to see"* ourselves as God sees us—seated in heavenly places through Christ!

Paul compares grace to riches. He goes on to say that grace is a gift of God and cannot be obtained on our own. We need to let go of so many things that have been passed down to us: reading the Bible out of obligation instead of joy; fasting too often; obeying the rules or thinking of God as the rule keeper; keeping every commandment; fasting to move God's hand; trying hard not to think of something negative; and others. Instead of *"counting it pure joy"* to be a child of God, we have tortured ourselves (and those around us) with these mindsets.

When God showed me His love and grace in a new way, my eyes were opened to His Kingdom all around me instead of the demonic and what was wrong. This paved the way for more heavenly and supernatural encounters. Give this a try, and watch what happens in your own life.

Many people long to have a visitation from an angel or Jesus. In my opinion, there can be an overemphasis in the charismatic and prophetic communities on experiencing a visitation. To be honest, I had very few spiritual experiences for most of my Christian life. When I started focusing more on developing the ability to "know Him better," I started moving in the Spirit of wisdom and revelation. I invite you to move into seeing and understanding the deeper things of God through the Holy Spirit.

Understanding the Supernatural

I love studying how things work, and have always wondered exactly how the amazing experiences happened that I read about in books or heard prophetic people talk about. Years ago, I had the opportunity to sit at a lunch table between two amazing men of faith: the late prophet Bob Jones and Rick Joyner, author of *The Final Quest*.

My burning question was: "How did you see all those prophetic visions? Were they in a dream state, an open vision, or pictures in your mind? Did the Holy Spirit just speak them to you, or what?" Before I could say a word, Bob Jones leaned over to me and answered the question I never said aloud: "Once you understand how God speaks, it doesn't matter how it comes to you."

I was in shock that he knew my thoughts, but his answer really cleared up a lot of things for me. I had been having dreams that seemed to "look very different" and felt significant. I had glimpses of visions a few times, but it was never anything dramatic. Bob helped me realize that God speaks to us in many ways. Oftentimes our own expectations keep us from understanding what God is saying. As we remove doubt and expectations about how we think it should happen, we can hear and experience Him in greater ways.

Remember the Job 33:14–17 principle:

> *For God does speak—now one way, now another—though no one perceives it. In a dream, in a vision of the night, when deep sleep falls on people as they slumber in their beds, he may speak in their ears and terrify them with*

> *warnings, to turn them from wrongdoing and keep them from pride.*

In other words, God is speaking all the time but we may not perceive it. He can impart revelation directly into our spirits, which we might pick up on later. God often bypasses our natural minds so that we do not get prideful.

Sometimes I have very dramatic encounters, but often they would probably seem quite "natural" to an observer. Most of the time "I just know" what God is saying or if there is an angel present. I have taken so many notes and practiced discerning so much that my spirit is sensitive to the spiritual atmosphere around me. This is why I am encouraging you to do the same.

This is a natural way of life for me, but it can be challenging at times. For instance, I often live out a prophetic word over a person, church, or city. This can be challenging because the demonic forces holding them back from fully entering God's destiny will attack me. Other times I live out the calling they have, and see the angels and assignments for them.

Because of this, I have trouble resting in people's homes. I often say I have enough trouble sleeping in my own home, let alone in the home of someone who is unaware of how the deep things of God's Kingdom work. I rest better in hotels because demons are not usually assigned to hotels, and I can more easily command things to leave. In someone's house though, when I command a demon to leave, it often tells me it has permission to be there through the assignment over the family. This is not an easy thing to tell a person at the breakfast table the next morning—especially a leader.

For the longest time, I thought I was crazy and did not understand this gift or these experiences. My wife has helped me stay balanced.

From Seeing Demons to Seeing Angels

I have had demonic encounters and was tormented terribly for most of my life. I have since learned that they come through several different sources. Now I spend a lot of time cutting off negative generational ties and releasing God's goodness over my life. I believe we need deliverance type of prayer; but if we focus too much on it, we miss the greater levels God wants for us. The Bible provides more descriptions and places a greater emphasis on God, Jesus, the Holy Spirit, and angels than on the demonic realm. This is where I choose to keep my focus as well.

A radical angelic encounter I had in 1991 took me years to understand. I have had many encounters with the Holy Spirit, but none like this. During a walk in the woods while camping, I came upon a place I had seen in a vision while praying the week before. There was no mistaking the power and presence of God I felt in that place. I was knocked to the ground, and though I could not see the angel with my eyes open, I could see it whenever I closed my eyes. I can still hear the words that it spoke directly into my spirit.

This angelic encounter gave me a very powerful message about things that were coming to my family, which would be a sign that these things would also come on the earth. For the longest time it bothered me that I had not physically seen the angel, but thirteen years later, all the things the angel told me actually took place, and I was permitted to release the prophetic word.

Even though the angelic encounter only lasted a few minutes, I received a massive amount of revelation from the Holy Spirit over the next two days while camping. It was as if I was hooked up to a direct line from Heaven. This was long before I became a pastor and teacher, and just a couple of years after I came out of the occult. Back then I did not understand how God spoke. But even though I did not realize the depth of what I had heard from God, I still took pages of notes.

What the angel told me was outside of our context of "time." The angel said, "Your mom is dead; tell your stepfather to stay in the church, and he will marry a godly woman." My mom was very much alive and my stepdad, Ray, was not even a Christian or in church at the time. But a few years later, my mom got sick and my stepdad gave his life to Jesus. When mom died in 1999, I told Ray what God had spoken to me. He stayed in the church, and in 2004 Ray married a godly woman. They are still serving God together.

God is outside of time. The Holy Spirit or an angel will often speak a message to you that has no context of time attached to it. This is a common reason people misunderstand the timing of prophetic words.

Hearing the Holy Spirit and Angels

In my encounter, I had an initial visitation from the angel and then the Holy Spirit continued to speak to me over the next few days. This is similar to an encounter Jesus' disciple Philip had with an angel:

> *Now an angel of the Lord* **said** *to Philip, "Go south to the road—the desert road—that goes down from Jerusalem to Gaza." So he started out, and on his way he met an Ethiopian eunuch, an important official in charge of all the treasury of the Kandake (which means "queen of the Ethiopians")* (Acts 8:26–27).

When Philip saw the chariot stopped along the road, *"The Spirit told Philip, 'Go to that chariot and stay near it'"* (Acts 8:29). Notice the encounter starts with an angel speaking to Philip and ends with the Holy Spirit continuing the instructions. The result was the man in the chariot received Jesus.

Sometimes we know we are encountering angels face to face, and other times it can seem as if we are dreaming or having a vision:

The night before Herod was to bring him to trial, Peter was sleeping between two soldiers, bound with two chains, and sentries stood guard at the entrance. Suddenly an angel of the Lord appeared and a light shone in the cell. He struck Peter on the side and woke him up. "Quick, get up!" he said, and the chains fell off Peter's wrists.

*Then the angel said to him, "Put on your clothes and sandals." And Peter did so. "Wrap your cloak around you and follow me," the angel told him. Peter followed him out of the prison, but **he had no idea that what the angel was doing was really happening; he thought he was seeing a vision**. They passed the first and second guards and came to the iron gate leading to the city. It opened for them by itself, and they went through it. When they had walked the length of one street, suddenly the angel left him.*

*Then Peter came to himself and said, "**Now I know without a doubt that the Lord has sent his angel** and rescued me from Herod's clutches and from everything the Jewish people were hoping would happen"* (Acts 12:6–11).

Notice in verse 9: *"Peter followed him out of the prison, but he had no idea that what the angel was doing was really happening; he thought he was seeing a vision."* Then in verse 10, *"the iron gate leading to the city ... opened for them by itself, and they went through it."* That was not a small garden gate, but a huge one made of iron. It would take more than a strong wind to blow that thing open!

When the angel disappeared in the middle of the street, Peter finally realized that all of it was really happening:

When this had dawned on him, he went to the house of Mary the mother of John, also called Mark, where many people had gathered and were praying. Peter knocked at the outer entrance, and a servant named Rhoda came to answer the door. When she recognized Peter's voice, she was so overjoyed she ran back without opening it and exclaimed, "Peter is at the door!" "You're out of your mind," they told her. When she kept insisting that it was so, they said, "It must be his angel" (Acts 12:12–15).

The fact that they were so ready to believe it was Peter's angel indicates angelic encounters were common, and we all have angels that can look like us. We will need to ask the Lord to open our spiritual eyes and ears so we can receive all that He has for us. The journey into the supernatural side of God will challenge you. There is no need to be afraid as we are learning to discern the real from the counterfeit!

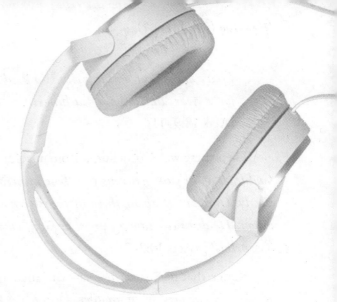

CHAPTER 15

Angels and More ~

The Bible is full of stories that describe amazing supernatural encounters. Before Jesus was born, Joseph almost divorced Mary because he thought she had been unfaithful to him.

> *But after he had considered this, an angel of the Lord appeared to him in a dream and said, "Joseph son of David, do not be afraid to take Mary home as your wife, because what is conceived in her is from the Holy Spirit"* (Matthew 1:20).

When Paul was in Corinth, God personally encouraged him to keep going, even though the religious leaders strongly opposed him:

> *One night the Lord spoke to Paul in a vision: "Do not be afraid; keep on speaking, do not be silent. For I am with you, and no one is going to attack and harm you, because*

> I have many people in this city." So Paul stayed in Corinth
> for a year and a half, teaching them the word of God
> (Acts 18:9–11).

Then there was Cornelius, a Roman soldier, who was "*devout and God-fearing; he gave generously to those in need and prayed to God regularly. One day at about three in the afternoon he [Cornelius] had a vision. He distinctly saw an angel of God, who came to him and said, 'Cornelius!'*" (Acts 10:2–3).

Notice that he "*distinctly*" saw the angel in this vision. God truly speaks "*in one way, or in another*" (Job 33:14 NKJV). Some supernatural experiences simply cannot be explained. As I speak at events and coach people about these things, the supernatural encounter stories start flying left and right. Many people have not had a place to share or anyone to help explain them.

As they share their close encounters of a "God kind," people ask, "What was the purpose of this experience?" Sometimes, we might not be able to identify a specific purpose. But even when they cannot be explained or understood, it's exciting just to "catch a glimpse" into the spiritual realm. Times like this might just be God showing that He cares about us and likes to surprise us.

The books of Ezekiel and Revelation contain some strange visions that, to this day, cannot be fully explained. Revelation can sometimes be strange and unexplainable; other times its meaning is obvious.

Philip and the Ethiopian

Right after Philip baptized the Ethiopian, Philip was literally, supernaturally transported from one place on earth to another. He vanished and then reappeared twenty to thirty miles away, possibly still soaked with lake water.

When they came up out of the water, the Spirit of the Lord suddenly took Philip away, and the eunuch did not see him again, but went on his way rejoicing. Philip, however, appeared at Azotus and traveled about, preaching the gospel in all the towns until he reached Caesarea (Acts 8:39–40).

Peter's Trance

About noon the following day as they were on their journey and approaching the city, Peter went up on the roof to pray. He became hungry and wanted something to eat, and while the meal was being prepared, he fell into a trance. He saw heaven opened and something like a large sheet being let down to earth by its four corners. It contained all kinds of four-footed animals, as well as reptiles and birds. Then a voice told him, "Get up, Peter. Kill and eat." "Surely not, Lord!" Peter replied. "I have never eaten anything impure or unclean." The voice spoke to him a second time, "Do not call anything impure that God has made clean" (Acts 10:9–15).

Within a matter of hours, Peter had the encounter with Cornelius. I am not sure we realize how radical this was. Cornelius was a Roman soldier and a Gentile (non-Jew). At the time, the Jewish people were calling them an abomination. Yet God was moving on them and filled them with the Holy Spirit.

Do not miss this: Peter had a supernatural encounter, God gave him the meaning, Peter responded, and it resulted in a major paradigm shift for the early church to not exclude anyone from the message of salvation through Jesus.

Counterfeit Versus Real

As you read about more of my personal supernatural encounters, keep in mind that for everything God releases, the enemy tries to counterfeit the same thing. Counterfeits, or false versions of God's supernatural, have caused people to be fearful of any encounters.

For example, transportations happen to various places on earth through the Holy Spirit. But a counterfeit is *astral-projection*, which is done through a spirit guide and not the Holy Spirit. Prophetic words can be counterfeited with psychic words, just like there are both angels and demons.

I have asked God to release an opening to the supernatural over you as you continue reading.

Staying Grounded

When we are talking about the supernatural things of God, it is important to stay grounded in the Bible. We are not trying to change the truth of who Jesus is. We must build our spiritual lives on the foundation that Jesus is the Son of God and He died for our sins. He rose from the dead and ascended into Heaven according to the prophetic Holy Scriptures from the Old Testament and the Jewish Torah.

God has manifested Himself in three forms, the Father, Son, and Holy Spirit, yet all are one God. There are angels of the Lord as well. We do not worship angels or pray to them. We pray to God the Father in the name (authority) of Jesus and through the power of the Holy Spirit. We should always ask God the Father and not try to contact angels or people who have died and are now in Heaven.

When God speaks to us or we experience something supernatural, it is important to ask the Lord for confirmation of it in the Bible. We need to test the spirits and all of our encounters.

Decrees from Heaven

On June 29, 2009, I was praying at home and experienced an extraordinary "open heaven" in my house. Suddenly, it was like I had a brief encounter of being in direct connection with God, and I knew His heart and how to pray. It went on for about thirty minutes. During the experience, I had a divine download of *all* the promises God had made to me that have never come to pass. Something rose up inside me, and I had sudden supernatural strength and authority to speak and command these promises into existence.

A short time later, I was standing and marveling at what had just happened. Suddenly, a piece of ancient-looking paper literally appeared in midair, dropped to the floor and disappeared. It happened so fast that I did not have time to take it all in. It was very real and was a parchment, with what appeared to be gold or bronze trim.

I was not able to make out any writing on it, as it went as fast as it came. God spoke to me that the paper was a "decree from Heaven" regarding the prayers that I had been praying. He told me that my prayers were heard, and He issued orders to carry them out.

> *I will proclaim the Lord's decree:* He said to me, "You are my son; today I have become your father. Ask me, and I will make the nations your inheritance, the ends of the earth your possession" (Psalm 2:7–8).

God has indeed issued decrees from Heaven for you to take hold of your inheritance. All the prophetic promises for your life are now unfolding. The enemy has responded with a counterattack to try to steal your spiritual identity. In response to this, God is now releasing the plan to overcome spiritual identity theft.

What you decide on will be done, and light will shine on your ways (Job 22:28).

Visions of the Next Day

The very next month, in July 2009, I had a dream that was more of a spiritual experience. In the natural, I was leaving for a ministry trip the next day to Bakersfield, California. That night, I was taken in the spirit to the meeting I was about to attend. I saw the church building and the people leading the meeting. The next day when I arrived at the church, everything was as it was in the encounter, down to the hairstyles of the leaders.

But more happened in the experience. I was instructed to assemble black, handheld electronic devices that looked like electric torches but required no electricity. They were powered by the Holy Spirit and would be used to do ministry at an entirely new level. As I screwed the handles to the torches, it created a sound in the spirit that was like no sound I have heard on earth. It had an electronic pitch and reverberated forever. The sound was so strange that it caused many Christians to get angry, and I was attacked by many of them who did not want to hear this new sound.

I understood that God was releasing a new sound and a new anointing that will be so radical, many Christians will be tempted to reject them. The torches and the sound were reserved for a generation and group of people who would take them and run with them to new levels of God's supernatural glory, unlike anything we have ever seen.

It was interesting to note that the very weekend this dream experience happened, news outlets announced that the largest oil field in Bakersfield was discovered. God used this to confirm that we are about to discover something new and very big in the spirit realm.

A few days later, I was back home in Santa Maria, California, telling my wife about the experience. At that very moment, we pulled up to a traffic light and saw two teenagers carrying a torch of fire running up the street yelling with joy. It looked like the Olympic torch with real fire, and it was happening in real life. God spoke to me that it is time to release the "torch bearers" who will take His light and love to the world like never before.

This is a prophetic word for now:

> *For I will pour water on the thirsty land, and streams on the dry ground; I will pour out my Spirit on your offspring, and my blessing on your descendants. They will spring up like grass in a meadow, like poplar trees by flowing streams. Some will say, "I belong to the Lord"; others will call themselves by the name of Jacob; still others will write on their hand, "The Lord's," and will take the name Israel* (Isaiah 44:3–5).

God is saving the best for last!

Mom's Angel

My mom was an amazing woman of God. She died in 1999, way before her time. I now operate in many of the spiritual gifts and callings she had. Ten years after mom died, I had an unusual supernatural experience with an angel. I was home alone and a strong presence of the Lord came into my house. I felt it in a certain area of the room, so I went closer to it and the presence felt like my mom!

This was really strange because it seemed as though I was feeling my dead mom's spirit. It totally freaked me out! On the other hand, it was comforting and full of God's love. Then this presence sat next to me on the couch. I recognized the feeling of my mom, but as I kept paying attention, I began to discern that this was *not* my mom, but an angel.

I felt a touch from the angel and it spoke into my spirit, from the outside in. It said, "I was just in the presence of your mother in Heaven, and it is her presence on me that you feel. The Lord has sent me here to impart to you the things that your mother has been praying about for you in Heaven."

WOW! This was radical! It explains why people sometimes say their dead grandmother or another family member has come to them. It is probably an angel that has been assigned to the family that has come, but they can feel their relative's presence on that angel because they have been with that angel! After journaling about the experience later, I realized the angel had touched my right arm and spoke into my right ear.

A few months later, I was in Ohio packing up my sister's house. My sister suffered from the same disease that took my mom, and I had to put her in a nursing home. So, I was cleaning out my older sister's stuff when I came across a letter from my mom to my sister from 1984, before my mom was sick. Mom wrote about an encounter she had with an angel.

At the time, she was working as a hostess at a restaurant. She said that "suddenly I felt a hand on my shoulder and I felt a whisper in my ear, and the voice that whispered into my ear told me to go and speak to a man sitting alone at a table."

As it turned out, the man was going through a difficult time and she was able to minister to him. She continued in the letter, "I will never forget that voice and that touch on my shoulder." As I was reading the letter, the presence of God came into my sister's apartment and the angel spoke to me, "That was me, and I have been with your family for a long time, and I am now assigned to you."

I now understand more about discerning the difference between the voice of the Holy Spirit and that of an angel. The Holy Spirit tends to speak to us internally, whereas angels will seem to come from the outside in. It does not matter if it is audible or not. The Holy Spirit resides in us, and angels come in and out of our lives. Begin to notice this happening in your life.

This Is Not Necromancy

Necromancy is a practice of communicating with the dead using a spirit guide, witchcraft, sorcery, or New Age practices. I just described having a supernatural encounter with seeing an angel who had been assigned to my mother in Heaven. This is not necromancy as I am not trying to communicate with my dead mother. I have never tried to connect with my mother outside of God showing me a vision similar to what I just shared.

It is safe and biblical to have visions from the Lord of what is happening in Heaven. It is important for us to pray to the Lord through the name of Jesus in the power of the Holy Spirit. Never try to contact the dead. Always ask the Lord for what you need.

On the Mount of Transfiguration, Jesus is seen speaking with Moses and Elijah. These are two people that were no longer on earth but were in Heaven.

Matthew 17:1–3 says, *"After six days Jesus took with him Peter, James and John the brother of James, and led them up a high mountain by themselves. There he was transfigured before them. His face shone like the sun, and his clothes became as white as the light. Just then there appeared before them Moses and Elijah, talking with Jesus.*

In the book of Hebrews, the great cloud of witnesses is mentioned in chapter 12. If you read chapter 11, you will see a list of those who were commended for their faith in the Lord. Then in Hebrews 12:1

it tells us that we are surrounded by this cloud of faith-filled witnesses who are praying for us from Heaven:

> *Therefore, since we are surrounded by such a great cloud of witnesses, let us throw off everything that hinders and the sin that so easily entangles.*

It is important to test every spirit and vision that we receive. Ask God to confirm what you are seeing and if it is from Him or not. Be cautious, especially if you are new to experiencing the supernatural side of God.

Mom's Promotion in Heaven

In 2010, I was sitting in a church listening to a speaker, and we entered into a ministry time at the end of the service. As I worshiped, the presence of the Lord came on me like fire. I knew it was the presence of a very powerful angel standing right in front of me. I held my hands out before me, and I felt the angel touching my hands.

When I closed my eyes, I could actually see the angel standing in front of me. I did not want to open my eyes because I did not want the experience to stop. The angel put its thumbs into the palms of my hands, and I could see into Heaven in real time. It was like watching a video monitor of what was happening in Heaven.

I saw a ceremony where my mom was receiving her crown of glory. It was the most awesome thing I have ever seen. Mom looked like Esther—that is the only thing I can say to describe her. She was wearing a long robe with a very long white train and had a three-dimensional thing on her head that was made up of swirling, colorful laser lights—her crown of glory.

There were angels standing around her, and they put a scepter into her hand. Now, two things about my mom—she was a jokester like me, and she could drive a stick-shift car. When the angels put the scepter in her hand, I saw her begin moving it around, all over the place. It made me think of her before she could drive a stick shift, and I laughed as I watched.

As she moved the scepter all around, wherever she would point it, things would light up. And as things in Heaven lit up, angels would respond with sounds or with singing. The angels standing with her, who had put the scepter into her hand, grabbed her hand and steadied it, showing her how to lean it toward the throne of God that was off in the distance.

As she moved the scepter and learned to lean it toward the throne, then the throne of God would light up in the distance. And as it would light up, resources from Heaven would be sent off according to the requests of her prayers and thoughts.

After the angels worked with her for a few minutes, and as I was watching in real time, suddenly my mom yelled, "Give it to Doug!" Instantly, because I had my hands stretched out, the angel in front of me placed the scepter in my hands. It was in the spiritual realm, but I could feel it in my hands. The presence of God was so awesome and it burned with love and authority.

Once it was in my hands, I suddenly "came to reality" and realized I was back in the meeting. I fell to the floor because the power was so strong. I had to be driven home, and was drunk in the spirit for days. To this day, when I hold out my hands, I can feel the burning of the scepter. I have a new authority in prayer because of this, and am very cautious over whom I speak this authority.

I have inherited several things from my mother, including her outreach prophetic gifts. I also inherited her Bible when she died—the one she had kept with her through her illness and throughout hospice care.

Well, after this particular Sunday morning, I went home and my mom's Bible was opened to Esther chapter 5. I had not opened it to that book. That chapter tells of Esther going before the throne of the king, knowing that if the king would lean his scepter toward her, she would have favor. That was an awesome encounter!

I want to remind you that you do not need to have dramatic encounters like I am talking about here. For years I have heard God in the ways that you and most others do. I am only sharing this with you to increase your faith for more and to prepare you for what is yet to come! Jesus said that you will do what He did and greater works if you believe (John 14:12).

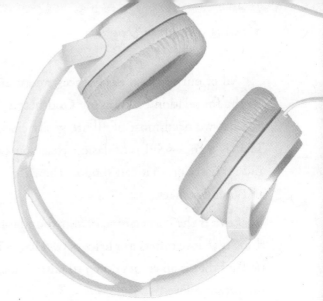

CHAPTER 16

More Supernatural Experiences ～——

We tend to think of Heaven as a place we go in the future when we die. Heaven is a very real place where the Lord is interacting with us all the time; but it is concealed behind a veil. Once in a while someone talks about encountering an angel or having a supernatural experience that cannot be explained.

Keep in mind the main principle and purpose of hearing God and experiencing the supernatural is found in Ephesians 1:17. I keep emphasizing this because it truly is the banner over my life and ministry. I have built all of my life's work in ministry on this foundation:

> *I keep asking that the God of our Lord Jesus Christ, the glorious Father, may give you the Spirit of wisdom and revelation, so that you may know him better* (Ephesians 1:17).

All of our spiritual experiences, and everything that we do, is laid on the foundation of knowing God better. When it comes down to it, what we need most of all are godly character, humility, and love. That is a rock-solid foundation that you can build an amazing life and ministry on that can support the weight of all kinds of situations and circumstances.

Love is the cornerstone of this foundation. Jesus said the greatest thing is to love others as He loves us. He reminds us through the apostle Paul that it all comes down to faith, hope, and love—and the most important is love.

Heaven opened over Jesus during His baptism:

> *When all the people were being baptized, Jesus was baptized too. And as he was praying, heaven was opened and the Holy Spirit descended on him in bodily form like a dove. And a voice came from heaven: "You are my Son, whom I love; with you I am well pleased"* (Luke 3:21–22).

Shortly after the baptism of Jesus and Heaven opened, Jesus prophesies that Nathaniel would see Heaven open and that he would see angels.

> *He then added, "Very truly I tell you, you will see 'heaven open, and the angels of God ascending and descending on' the Son of Man"* (John 1:51).

This is similar to the experience that Jacob had in Genesis 28. He dreamed that he saw Heaven open and the Lord spoke to him. The Bible is full of these types of encounters. Once you understand how God speaks and how the Kingdom operates, you can actually live under an open heaven wherever you go. What I mean is that you can get connected with God and hear and experience Him more clearly.

Example in the Bible

In Matthew 17, Jesus took Peter, James, and John up on a mountain where they had a supernatural encounter. Suddenly Jesus was transformed from His human body into His glorified form.

Matthew 17:2–3,5 says:

> *There he was transfigured before them. His face shone like the sun, and his clothes became as white as the light. Just then there appeared before them Moses and Elijah, talking with Jesus. ... While he was still speaking, a bright cloud covered them, and a voice from the cloud said, "This is my Son, whom I love; with him I am well pleased. Listen to him!"*

Wow, that must have been a radical encounter for them all. Peter, James, and John got a glimpse into the heavenly realm that is around us all. Peter said later in 2 Peter 1:16–18 that he was an eyewitness of this and he encourages us to stay grounded, trusting Jesus and His majesty.

South Africa Angels

When I went to Cape Town, South Africa, I had five days of encounters that were very powerful. After our meetings, I would go back to my hotel room and be up half the night, or I would be taken places in the spirit.

One night, I had an encounter that was a lot like Peter's in Acts 12, where he did not know if it was a vision or if the angel was real. When I laid down on my bed, I was suddenly back in California and found myself driving down Highway 101, which runs through the town where I was living at the time. I was trying to figure out if this was really happening to me, or if I was having a dream or a vision. Whatever it was, it felt completely real!

As I was driving down the 101, I looked over and saw a group of about twelve California Department of Transportation workers on the side of the road. They were all bent over at the same angle, scooping things up and putting them into bags. They all turned their heads at the same time, looked directly at me, and locked eyes with me. In that moment, their faces turned into angelic faces with red eyes that looked like laser beams—and the fear of God hit me.

They all went back to work with their faces turned back down. The Holy Spirit spoke to me that these were *gathering angels: "And he will send his angels and gather his elect from the four winds, from the ends of the earth to the ends of the heavens"* (Mark 13:27). I saw that they were gathering small balls of white light, which were people's souls. I was told these were people who had been discarded, overlooked, or wounded by the church. But these gathering angels had come to scoop them up to be used by God.

While I was still in the encounter, I found myself back in my own home in California. I was shaking because the presence of God was so strong, and I was blown away by what I had seen. My doorbell rang, and I answered to find two angels literally standing at the door. One of them was dressed like a jester, and the other was wearing work clothes. I knew I was being assigned a comedy angel (laughter is medicine for the soul; see Proverbs 17:22 NKJV) and a worker angel to help me get things done. Then I was back in my room in South Africa.

I now do stand-up comedy as a means of sharing God's love and ministering to people. In fact, it was right after this encounter that my comedy went to a whole new level. People have received financial and physical healing at my events just by having fun.

Putting My Angels to Work

After a week of amazing encounters in South Africa, they continued once I returned home. On the very first day back home in California, I noticed that the presence of angels was still very strong. I had amazing quiet times and received a lot of revelation. A few days into it, I sensed that the angels I had encountered in South Africa were now with me in California. I asked God, "What do I do?" He answered, "Well, put them to work." I did not even know I could do that!

I really prayed about it for a day, then made my list and asked God to assign the angels to tasks. The next day, I woke up and there were no angels in my house! Their absence felt almost like being cold. I asked God, "Where are all the angels?" The Holy Spirit answered me, "Well, you put them to work. That's why they're not here." Then I understood that angels come to us, and when they get their assignments they literally leave and go to work.

About a week later, I was going through an especially difficult time. One night the angels started showing up again in my bedroom. I could not see them, but I could feel their presence. At times, I could see a light out of the corner of my eye, other times I saw shadows. I sat up in bed and asked them, "Why are you here? What's going on?"

As usual, the angels spoke directly into my spirit and said, "We do not have an assignment for you right now. You are moving into a new season in your life, and we do not have an assignment to protect you. But we are doubling up on assignments and rendezvousing in your bedroom at night." I thought, *Wow, this is interesting.*

I was receiving so much revelation simply because these angels were meeting in my bedroom in the middle of the night. It was funny that I would wake up and say out of nowhere, "There's something new in Detroit!" Stuff like that. I would not even know what it was about, except that the angels were rendezvousing in my bedroom in the middle of the night. Later, God assigned angels to me that have helped me get into a new place of maturity. I am sure that is why my blog articles on my website from 2009 are full of revelation. My life has not been the same since.

Promoted to Prophet

I want to share with you a major spiritual encounter I had that will help you understand more about what I am talking about. It came in the form of a dream, but it seemed to be more than that. This was a supernatural encounter with the Lord.

The term *Days of Awe* refers to the time between the Jewish holidays of Rosh Hashanah and Yom Kippur. To observant Jews, Yom Kippur (also known as the *Day of Atonement)* is considered the most holy day of the year. Although we are not under the Law of Moses, God still operates on the Jewish calendar. It is during the Days of Awe that God examines our lives for the purposes of promotion.

I would like to share with you a radical encounter I had the day before Yom Kippur, September 16, 2010, when I was promoted into a higher level of the prophetic. The spiritual experience I had was to tell me that this was going on in my life and that I was also going to have to walk out a season of testing. This was part of what I went through to grow into the spiritual governmental authority of a prophet. I don't consider the gifts and callings from God to be mere titles which are popular these days. They are more like a function.

> *So Christ himself gave the apostles, the prophets, the evangelists, the pastors and teachers, to equip his people for works of service, so that the body of Christ may be built up* (Ephesians 4:11–12).

As you have read in this book, the prophet has a function in the community and Church to bring God's words and wisdom to people. Based on how we respond to the testing God brings us along the way, we can grow into a place where our words carry more authority and actually create or change things instead of just announcing what God is saying. There is no set time limit, but for most people I know, it has taken fifteen years or more to move into becoming a seasoned prophet, someone God can entrust with authority because they have learned to love others as opposed to just worrying about God's words being received.

My 2010 Promotional Experience

September 16, 2010, was the day before Yom Kippur. I went to sleep and was taken into a very vivid dream-like spiritual experience. These types of experiences are usually more than a dream. I consider them visions or encounters similar to what Peter experienced in Acts 10 when he saw the sheet come down from Heaven. Or in Acts 12 when Peter was having an encounter with an angel that literally broke him out of prison but he had no idea it was real until later on.

> *Peter followed him out of the prison, but he had no idea that what the angel was doing was really happening; he thought he was seeing a vision* (Acts 12:9).

I was standing in a waiting room alone and I knew this was the room for those who were waiting to be promoted. I realized that I had been there many times before but was never chosen for a promotion. Then a Jewish rabbi/priest came into the room and said, "You're next." I said, "Who, me?" And he asked, "Do you have your ticket?" I did not; I must have tossed it away when I saw that I was not being promoted. He indicated it was okay and pointed to a board on the wall behind me. My name was the last one and I was number seven to be promoted into something major for that year.

The priest seemed tired and overworked as if he had a lot of people to process. He was a bit short in his words and had a sarcastic tone to his voice. He was wearing a black Hasidic-style suit and he had a grey beard. Then he looked over his glasses and murmured, "You have no idea who you are, do you?" In his hand was a file folder about my life, and I was catching on to the idea that I was up for a major promotion, which took me by surprise. He was looking through my file and said, "You need more communion between now and Yom Kippur." In reality, Yom Kippur began the next day, September 17–18; but in the spiritual realm, it was not necessarily literal communion, or literally the next day that he was speaking of. God is outside of time, so things we hear might not be literal.

I followed the priest to a tank that looked like a baptismal pool. He went behind a wall and then he emerged from a door and was standing on a platform over the pool that I was in. But now he was wearing a white priestly robe with jewels and gold inlay. He was holding a book open ready to perform a "Rite of Passage" that was going to be my invitation into the promotional process.

I looked down at the water in the tank and it was dirty with a half-used bar of soap from the guy who had been promoted before me. I was thinking that the guy must have had a rough time, and I was concerned about myself and hoping that it would not be that difficult for me. The priest apologized for the water and flushed the tank and it filled instantly with fresh clean water. After he read the Rite of Passage over me, he dunked me in the water, and then the scene changed.

I am now in the future and I am standing on a narrow, silver platform that led to a door of a silver building that looked like a jetway. I knew that the priest was inside the door waiting for me. I had to walk the narrow walkway and go inside the door. Once inside I was going to have to do something that would be a difficult sacrifice for me. I was instructed by the Holy Spirit that I would need to make an ultimate sacrifice in my life.

The sacrifice was symbolic of having to deal with things in my own life to get into this new place. This would be an offering to the Lord; and after I did it, I would have a meal with the priest and the Lord as a celebration for my promotion. I came out of the experience shaken and the awesomeness of God filled my bedroom.

What Happened Next

That was such an awesome experience, but at the same time I was still walking through a rough season in my life. What happened after the promotional experience in September 2010 was actually opposite of what I expected. I thought I would begin to operate in a greater level of the prophetic and people would receive the prophecies I had been releasing for a number of years. But indeed the ways of the Lord are often opposite to ours. I walked through several years of some of the most difficult trials and times of my life.

After these experiences, the Lord was faithful and He gave me supernatural strategies for our ministry and others to get out of debt and prepare for the revival that is coming. I wish someone would have shared these things with me years ago. It would have saved me a lot of pain and rejection. Because of my higher calling as a prophet, I was required to walk through some fiery times. But I would not trade any of it because I now have a deeper relationship with the Lord. It also opened the door for me to help millions of people hear God's voice and come to Jesus!

Get ready to receive more! God is faithful and He is going to pour out His Spirit and we can all know Him more and see Him bring His purposes to earth!

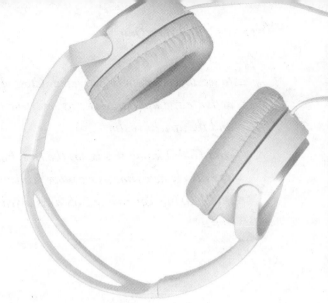

Closing Prayer

I am honored that you took the time to read and work through this book. I am praying that God will open the heavens over you and activate your ability to hear Him at a deeper level.

God, I pray for an open heaven over the person who is reading this right now. Father, bless this friend. Even though we may not have met, we are connected in the spirit. We are one body together.

Friend, I pray for dreams, visions, open heaven experiences, and supernatural encounters to flow over you right now. I pray for your eyes to open to the spiritual realm around you, and to the goodness that God has given to you through Jesus Christ.

Father, I thank You for giving us greater authority so that we can love and lift up each other. I speak that the ability to see angels would be activated. Close off the demonic and activate the angels. Make us sensitive to the Holy Spirit and the angelic realm.

And God, I know this is not the end, but the beginning of an entirely new time as we move forward and grow deeper into hearing Your voice 365 days a year. In Jesus' name, amen.

About the Author

Doug Addison is the founder and president of InLight Connection. Doug is a prophetic speaker, author and coach. He is best known for his *Daily Prophetic Words* and *Spirit Connection* webcast, podcast and blog. Doug's message of love, hope and acceptance reaches people around the world! His powerful, lighthearted style of teaching and coaching helps open people to discover their spiritual identity and personal destiny as they experience God's supernatural love and power. He and his wife Linda live in Los Angeles, California where they are impacting the arts and entertainment and media industries.

Contact Information

InLight Connection

PO Box 7049

Santa Maria, CA 93456

Phone: 805-346-1122

Email: help@DougAddison.com

Website: DougAddison.com

OTHER BOOKS BY DOUG ADDISON

Prophetic Forecast Volume 1

Prophetic Forecast Volume 2

Prophetic Forecast Volume 3

Understand Your Dreams Now: Spiritual Dream Interpretation

Discovering the Supernatural: Interacting With the Angelic and Heavenly Realms in Your Daily Life

Prophecy, Dreams, and Evangelism: Revealing God's Love Through Divine Encounters

God Spoke, Now What?: Activating Your Prophetic Word

Night Dreams Reveal Your Life Dreams

How to Hear God Clearly for Yourself

4 Powerful Keys That Change Your Life

Write a Book Quickly

Spiritual Identity Theft Exposed

How to Flip Your Financial Future

Experience a personal revival!

Spirit-empowered content from today's top Christian authors delivered directly to your inbox.

Join today!
lovetoreadclub.com

Inspiring Articles
Powerful Video Teaching
Resources for Revival

Get all of this and so much more, e-mailed to you twice weekly!

LOVE TO READ CLUB
by **D DESTINY IMAGE**